# Reading Bridge™
## 6th grade

Written by:

# Dr. Leland Graham
## and
# Darriel Ledbetter

**Project Directors:**     Michele D. Van Leeuwen
                                Scott G. Van Leeuwen

**Creative & Marketing Director:**     George Starks

**Product Development & Design Director**     Dante J. Orazzi

# Reading Bridge™
# 6th Grade

For more information write or call:
Rainbow Bridge Publishing
332 West Martin Lane, PO Box 571470
Salt Lake City, UT 84157-1470
801-268-8887
www.rainbowbridgepub.com

**Original Cover Art:**
Joe Flores

**Copy Editors and/or Proofreaders:**
Debbie Armstrong, Laura Armstrong, Angela Erickson, Dante Orazzi, George Starks, Dave Thompson, Carol VanLeeuwen, Leisel Vaughntrap, Kirsten Wille, Dixon

**Contributing Writers:**
George Starks and Kirsten Willie

**Graphic Design, Illustration and Layout:**
Thomas Dyches, Dante Orazzi and Jeffrey Whitehead

**The authors would like to gratefully acknowledge the assistance and suggestions of the following persons:**
William Baker, Randy Britton, Harriett Cook, Becky Lee, Beverly Moody, Dan Payne, and John Spilane


Printed by Press America in the U.S.A.

Printing History:
First Printing 1999
Second Printing 2000


ISBN: 1-887923-13-6


Printed in the United States of America
10  9  8  7  6  5  4  3  2  1

# Table of Contents

**Prepares Students For Standardized Achievement Tests**

# Introduction

The **Reading Bridge** series is designed to improve and motivate students' reading. This book has been developed to provide sixth grade students practical skill-based exercises in the areas of inferences, main ideas, cause and effect, fact and opinion, and figurative language. The purpose of this book is to familiarize students with the kinds of reading tasks they will encounter on a daily basis. Furthermore, reading will enrich and facilitate their lives as young adults in an ever-changing world that has information readily available but only if they learn to take advantage of and appreciate reading.

The stories, poems and essays in this collection are each accompanied by exercises that address reading skills. Each story, poem or essay has been written so that students at the sixth grade level can read it successfully. The carefully thought-out questions will help your students learn to think, inquire, create, imagine, respond and in some instances, do research to learn more about a specific topic.

The **Capitalization and Grammar Guide** found at the back of the book has been included to help students better understand common grammar found in day-to-day reading.

**Reading Bridge** adapts to any teaching situation whether at home or in the classroom. It can be used in many different ways. For instance:

✔ **For at home practice:** this series is ideal to supplement or extend school work and home school reading programs.

✔ **For the entire class:** this series can be used for intensive reinforcement of reading skills or to simply supplement a basal reading program.

✔ **For reading groups:** this series will provide skills practice at appropriate levels, and the reading exercises become progressively more challenging.

✔ **For individual use:** this series will help build a completely individualized program.

# Use Your Dictionary!!!

The English language is made up of thousands and thousands and thousands of words; so many words that it would be impossible for you to know what every single one of these words means! But wait! Just because you come across a word in this book, or somewhere else, that may be unfamiliar to you, does not mean that you should ignore it or give up on learning its meaning.

Instead, use a dictionary to learn the meaning of the word you don't know. You'll get better scores on the exercises in this book. More importantly, you'll expand your knowledge base and become a better communicator because you'll be able to both express yourself and understand other people more clearly!

**Dic • tion • ar • y, n. 1.** a book of alphabetically listed words in a language, with definitions, pronunciations, and other information about the words

# 6th Grade Reading List

**Alexander, Lloyd**
Book of Three
High King
Drackenberg Adventure
Illyrian Adventure
Jedera Adventure

**Alphin, Elaine Marie**
The Ghost Cadet

**Armstrong, William H.**
Sounder

**Banks, Lynne Reid**
The Return of the Indian
The Secret of the Indian

**Bellairs, John**
The Treasure of Alpheus Winterborn

**Biesty, Stephen**
Stephen Biesty's Incredible Cross-Sections

**Billingsley, Franny**
Well Wished

**Brown, Susan M.**
You're Dead David Borelli

**Byars, Betsy**
After the Goat Man
Pinballs
Cracker Jackson
Cybil War
The Midnight Fox

**Cooper, Susan**
The Grey King
Silver on the Tree

**Coville, Bruce**
Jeremy Thatcher, Dragon Hatcher
The Skull of Truth

**Creech, Sharon**
Absolutely Normal Chaos

**Dahl, Roald**
Matilda

**Fleischman, Sid**
The 13th Floor:A Ghost Story

**Franklin, Kristine L.**
Lone Wolf

**George, Jean Craighead**
The Fire Bug Connection
Julie of the Wolves
My Side of the Mountain
On the Far Side of the Mountain

**Greer, Gery**
This Island Isn't Big Enough for The Four of Us

**Jacques, Brian**
Redwall

**Jennings, Paul**
Uncovered!: Weird, Weird Stories

**Konigsburg, E.L.**
From The Mixed Up Files of Mrs. Basil E.
Frankweiler

**Lewis, C.S.**
The Magician's Nephew
Prince Caspian
The Voyage of the Dawn Treader

**Levine, Gail Carson**
Ella Enchanted

**Lowry, Lois**
Number The Stars

**Le Guin, Ursula K.**
The Farthest Shore

**Lowry, Lois**
The Giver

**McKay, Hilary**
The Amber Cat

**McKinley, Robin**
The Blue Sword

# 6th Grade Reading List

**Naylor, Philips Reynolds**
Alice In-Between
Alice In Rapture, Sort of
All But Alice
Reluctantly Alice
The Bodies In The Besseledorf Hotel
Bernie and the Besseledorf Ghost
The Boys Start the War
The Girls Get Even
The Fear Place
Shiloh

**O'Brien, Robert C.**
Mrs. Frisby and The Rats of NIMH

**O'Dell, Scott**
Sing Down The Moon
The Black Pearl

**Patterson, Katherine**
Bridge to Terabithia
Great Gilly Hopkins

**Paulsen, Gary**
Brian's Winter

**Peck, Robert Newton**
Soup's Goat
Soup and Me
Soup On Ice
Soup On Wheels

**Pevsner, Stella**
Me, My Goat, And My Sister's Wedding

**Rappaport, Doreen**
Escape From Slavery: Five Journeys To Freedom

**Roberts, Willo Davis**
View From The Cherry Tree
Who Invited The Undertaker

**Rocklin, Joanne**
For Your Eyes Only!

**Ruckman, Ivy**
No Way Out

**Sachar, Louis**
There's A Boy in the Girls' Bathroom

**Seidler, Tor**
Mean Margaret

**Snyder, Zilpha Keatley**
Velvet Room

**Soto, Gary**
Baseball in April and Other Stories

**Speare, Elizabeth George**
Sign of the Beaver
The Witch of Blackbird Pond

**Spinelli, Jerry**
The Library Card
Wringer

**Taylor, Theodore**
Timothy of the Cay

**Ullman, James R.**
Banner in the Sky

**Wardlaw, Lee**
101 Ways to Bug Your Parents

**White, E.B.**
Trumpet Of The Swan

**Winthrop, Elizabeth**
The Castle in the Attic

**Voight, Cynthia**
Homecoming

**Yep, Laurence**
Dragongate

**Zindel, Paul**
The Pigman and Me

# Incentive Contract

In • cen'tive, n. 1. Something that urges a person on. 2. Enticing. 3. Encouraging 4. That which excites to action or moves the mind.

## Below, List Your Agreed-Upon Incentive for Each Story Group

**Student's Signature**                              **Parent, Teacher, or Guardian Signature**

_____                    _____

### Place a ✔ after each story & exercise upon completion

| Page | Story & Exercise Title | ✔ | Page | Story & Exercise Title | ✔ |
|------|------------------------|---|------|------------------------|---|
| 8 | My New Companion | | 49 | The Canoe Trip | |
| 10 | The Farm | | 51 | The Turn Of Her Life | |
| 12 | Mountain Reminisce | | 52 | Journal On Our Trip To N.Y.C. | |
| 14 | Thoraya | | 54 | The Pond | |
| 15 | Christmas in a Grocery Store | | 56 | New School | |
| 18 | Scarecrow | | 58 | All I Can See | |
| 20 | Granddad | | 59 | The Canopy | |
| 22 | An Ode To a Pond | | 61 | My Favorite Spot | |
| 23 | Lady of the Harbor | | 62 | My English Journal | |
| 25 | Reflections on Pinewood Lake | | 64 | A Visit | |

**My Incentive Is**                                    **My Incentive Is**

| Page | Story & Exercise Title | ✔ | Page | Story & Exercise Title | ✔ |
|------|------------------------|---|------|------------------------|---|
| 27 | The Scare in the Mountains | | 66 | The Secret | |
| 29 | A Dream | | 68 | Four-Wheeler Fishing Trip | |
| 30 | The Calf | | 70 | The Apple | |
| 32 | Tiger Town | | 70 | Night Shade | |
| 34 | Boom Boom's Turkey Farm | | 72 | Billy and the Butterfly | |
| 36 | Mom at Bat | | 75 | The Sky | |
| 39 | The Game | | 77 | An Exercise in Futility | |
| 40 | An Essay on the Grand Canyon | | 79 | Dozing | |
| 42 | Help! I'm Lost | | 81 | Friends | |
| 44 | The Race | | 84 | Fate Over Chocolate Pie | |
| 47 | What Really Happened to Jack? | | 89 | Focus | |

**My Incentive Is**                                    **My Incentive Is**

# My New Companion

I remember the day we met. It was my ninth birthday. My mom and I were pulling into the driveway when I saw it, my new **companion**, standing there half visible behind my dad. I didn't need to see the whole thing to know what it was. It was beautiful! Instantly I fell in love with the worn yellow seat and the polished chrome handlebars, which glowed with blinding luster in the afternoon sun. My eyes lit up, and without hesitation I climbed aboard.

It took me a while to feel completely comfortable with my new companion, but before two weeks passed we were inseparable. Every day we would ride, rain or shine. And it was on one of these days that we faced our biggest challenge.

It was a bright, sunny day. My companion and I were cruising along a relatively flat and well-paved street two blocks from my house when we encountered a group of boys who had set up a ramp. I stopped pedaling and paused to watch as the boys took turns riding their bikes up the ramp, which propelled them straight into the air before they landed back onto the pavement with a loud clank and clatter. The object was to catch as much air as possible.

When a few of the boys in the group finally noticed me, they signaled for me to come over. "Hey there," said a red-headed kid with lots of freckles as I approached the group, "why don't you give it a try?" The thought of trying to "catch air" myself hadn't crossed my mind, but the redhead persisted, so I lined myself up to take the plunge.

My palms began to sweat and my heart pounded as I contemplated the possibility that I might crash. The more I thought about what I was doing, the more frightened I became. Knowing that if I didn't do something soon I would become completely paralyzed with fear, I climbed onto the yellow seat, grabbed the handlebars, and let myself go. Without giving it much thought, I started pedaling faster and faster, and before I knew it, I launched into the sky!

It took nearly six weeks for my broken arm to heal. But for four of those weeks, I could still ride my bike. And with the all the practice I've had, the ramp no longer poses a problem for me and my companion. I even made a whole new group of friends who all signed my cast. The doctor let me keep it as a token of my courage! I learned that whether you're learning to ride a bike, meeting new friends or taking on a new challenge, overcoming your fear is the first step. And once you do, there's very little to stop you from achieving your goal!

# READING CHALLENGE

**After reading "My New Companion," answer the following questions.**

1. **What is the main idea of the story?**
   A. Learning to ride a bike is fun.
   B. It is great to get presents from parents.
   C. It is good to try to overcome fear.
   D. A companion like a dog is great.

2. **What is a synonym for the word <u>companion</u>?**
   A. bike          B. enemy          C. parents          D. partner

3. **Which one of the following statements is an opinion, not a fact?**
   A. It was the writer's ninth birthday.
   B. Bikes with yellow seats are the best.
   C. The writer's companion is a bike.
   D. The bike has a worn, yellow seat.

4. **Which of the following events happened last?**
   A. It took nearly six weeks for my broken arm to heal.
   B. Instantly I fell in love with the worn yellow seat and the polished chrome handlebars...
   C. My palms began to sweat and my heart pounded...
   D. My companion and I were cruising along...

5. **In this story, the word <u>companion</u> means**
   A. a person who works for a large company.
   B. a partner, friend or associate.
   C. transportation.
   D. the part of the bicycle that you steer with.

Remember, if you don't know what a word means, look it up in a dictionary! You'll do better in the exercises!

RBP

# The Farm

I was eleven when my folks decided that my sister and I needed to spend some time with our great-grandmother Mawmaw. It was mandated that we should begin packing right now for an overnight visit. Neither one of us wanted to go.

It had been so long since we had been there. We couldn't even remember anything about her. Just thinking about Mawmaw sent visions of sheer boredom, listening to her go on and on about the past. We couldn't imagine sitting on the front porch watching Mawmaw creaking back and forth, forth and back in the old gray green rocking chair, while her set of teeth are soaking in a dish on top of a discarded opened book beside her cloudy bifocals. It sounded like excruciating punishment.

We tried everything we could think of to get out of going. We pretended to be sick. We pouted. My sister even threw a temper tantrum over it to no avail. Our parents' patience ran out. Before we knew it we were packed and into the car. Down the endless, tiresome road we went. Mother tried to make the trip shorter by humoring us into believing that we would enjoy ourselves if we just gave it a chance. "Oh, sure," I thought.

Mawmaw met us at the door with her toothless smile, a hug and a squeeze that left us gasping for air. She exclaimed over how much we had grown. Mom and Dad visited for a while before they had to leave to drive all the way back to the city. I pled with Mom one last time before she turned away and left. closing the door behind her.

Mawmaw showed us around the place and told us about a collie she had recently adopted named Laddie. She wanted us to meet her. I informed Mawmaw, that since all my dolls were named Sally, I was going to call the Collie Sally as well. To my surprise, she agreed and Jennifer and I played with the dog all day long. We gave her cornbread, water, and even grapes and strawberries from Mawmaw's garden. The strawberries tasted great, "Like sugar wrapped in the sunlight," Mawmaw said.

Mawmaw doesn't have most modern conveniences. She gets her water from a well and bathes in an old tin tub. And if you have to go to the bathroom at Mawmaw's house, then you have to walk outside and visit the outhouse. Jennifer and I didn't really miss the comforts of home and we soon started to enjoy living like Mawmaw. That night, the three of us lay in her big feather bed while she told stories of her childhood on the farm.

Neither Jennifer nor I ever forgot that visit, and during the rest of our childhood years, we made many return visits. But as we grew older, we saw Mawmaw less and less. She has passed on now. Her loss was hard for us at first. But now, when I ride by the old farm, the good time memories flash before me and leave me with a smile on my face.

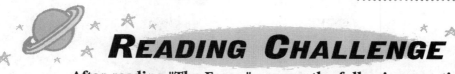

# READING CHALLENGE

### After reading "The Farm," answer the following questions.

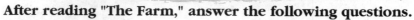

1. **Which one of the following is an inference?**
   A. The speaker changed her mind about old people.
   B. Mawmaw had no teeth.
   C. Old people tell boring stories.
   D. The dog's name is Laddie and Sally.

2. **One of the following expressions is a simile. Which one?**
   A. there is nothing more tedious for an eleven-year-old
   B. Mawmaw met us at the door with a toothless smile
   C. the strawberries tasted like sugar wrapped in the sunlight
   D. the comforts of home

3. **What part of speech is the underlined word in the sentence, "Mawmaw showed us around the <u>place</u> and told us about a Collie she had recently adopted named Laddie."**
   A. noun          B. pronoun          C. verb          D. adjective

4. **For how many years did Mawmaw live on the farm?**
   A. is not given          B. 20 yrs          C. 50 yrs          D. 60 yrs

5. **Who is Mawmaw?**
   A. mother                          C. grandmother
   B. great-grandmother               D. neighbor

6. **Why is Laddie capitalized?**
   A. because it is a proper adjective          C. because it is a proper noun
   B. because it is a proper pronoun            D. should not be capitalized

7. **Is the following statement true or false?**
   **"Jennifer and I left the next morning with the same attitude about elderly people."**

8. **This story is told by a/an _____ year old girl.**
   A. eleven          B. thirteen          C. twelve          D. fourteen

9. **What is the subject of the following sentence?**
   **"during the rest of our childhood years, we made many return visits."**
   A. years          B. rest          C. we          D. childhood

RBP

# Mountain Reminisce

As I sat exhausted on the **trail**,
I noticed a squirrel with a big fluffy **tail**.
The very sight of him made me smile,
For I knew he'd be my friend all the while.

When I watched my little friend work,
I stood up with a sudden jerk.
My friend had **inspired** me, indeed he had.
He'd shown me that it wasn't so bad.

I'd become tired and had stopped to rest,
But the squirrel was so **tireless**; he passed the test!
He reminded me to never quit,
Just keep on going, and always remember it!

So I started to climb again with a new surge of strength
As I followed the trail up the mountain's length.
I later grew tired again as I climbed,
But I did not stop and I did not look behind.

I had to make it; I knew that I could,
And I knew that I would.
Then at last I reached the top,
And not until then did I let myself stop.

When I took a look around,
I could hardly believe what I had found.
It was the most wonderful sight I had ever seen,
And then I felt as glorious as a queen.

I had not stopped, and now I was glad,
For, if I had, I would have later been mad.
But I was especially thankful for my little squirrel friend,
Who had taught me to push 'til the very end!

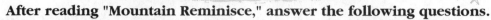

# READING CHALLENGE
### After reading "Mountain Reminisce," answer the following questions.

1. **The main idea of the poem "Mountain Reminisce" is**
   A. that it is fun to hike in the mountains.
   B. that one should never give up when working toward a goal.
   C. that it is not fun to have animals as friends.
   D. that one should be careful climbing in the woods.

2. **What is the term for words like <u>trail</u> and <u>tail</u> that sound alike at the end of poetic lines (see lines 1 and 2 in the poem)?**
   A. simile          B. alliteration          C. metaphor          D. rhyme

3. **The word <u>reminisce</u> in the title means**
   A. retreat.          B. adventure.          C. remember.          D. friend.

4. **"...I felt as glorious as a queen." What form of figurative language is used in this line of poetry?**
   A. simile          B. personification          C. metaphor          D. pun

5. **In line 10, what is the antonym for <u>tireless?</u>**
   A. energetic          B. tired          C. unending          D. stimulating

6. **The squirrel in this poem is being personified as a/an**
   A. mountain.          B. enemy.          C. woods.          D. friend.

7. **The setting for this poem is a/an**
   A. valley.          B. ocean.          C. mountain.          D. cabin.

8. **"My friend had <u>inspired</u> me, indeed he had..." Choose a word that means the same as the underlined word.**
   A. encouraged          B. trusted          C. insulted          D. disheartened

RBP

# THORAYA

The last of the sun's rays penetrated the clouds, leaving specks of gold on the heather-covered hills.  As Thoraya wound her way up the hillside, the wind blew in short gusts, causing the heather to sway back and forth in waves like a lazy river on a crisp summer day.  Today was Thoraya's third day in a new school in a foreign land.  She stepped lightly, and once at the top, her eyes scanned the horizon.  With her heart heavy and sore, Thoraya buried herself in a pile of nearby hay and wept.

The harsh voices of the unruly American school children echoed in her head.  Night began to fall and Thoraya's gaze moved slowly upward, coming to rest on the departing clouds.

Today Thoraya was painfully aware of how different she was from the other kids at school. She had just turned twelve and because of her country's customs, she had to wear a long, black dress called an abaya, and a scarf to cover her hair.  In Saudi Arabia, this was expected of a girl her age.  But in her new country, this seemed very strange.  However, her name was mostly the source of the children's mockery.  As she wept, she fell into a deep sleep.

She dreamt of her school in Saudi Arabia where all her friends thought her name was beautiful. "How could they possibly fancy a name that means chandelier?" she thought to herself.  "Why couldn't my parents have named me Sara? It's much more beautiful."

As she dreamt, a gust of cool wind swept her scarf from her head, waking her and leaving her with a slight chill.  She jumped up to retrieve the scarf and gasped at the sight before her.  The sky had turned pitch black, but illuminating the endless night were tiny, glowing stars that shone like specks of glitter on a swatch of black velvet.  Her head bent back and arms raised, Thoraya spun round and round.  The stars' reflections made a rainbow of colors like the prism of a chandelier.  The faster she spun, the more colors she could see.  Seeing this, she was struck by the significance and beauty of her name.  And from that day forth, she was never ashamed of it again.

## READING CHALLENGE

After reading "Thoraya," answer the following questions.

1.  **From what part of the world might one suppose that Thoraya has come?**
    A. America          B. South America     C. Europe          D. Middle East

2.  **What does Thoraya's name mean?**
    A. light            B. chandelier        C. Arabia          D. lovely one

3.  **What is the main idea?**
    A. Don't be ashamed of who you are or where you are from.
    B. Enjoy every day at school.
    C. If you move to a new country, forget your old country.
    D. Make new friends quickly at school.

14                                    *Total Correct*_____

# Christmas in a Grocery Store

This Christmas, I didn't receive as many gifts as I usually do, because my family and I helped other families who couldn't afford to celebrate the holidays. Many families can't even afford a Christmas dinner, which is why my dad and I donated and delivered groceries to needy families this year. I guess I've always known the true meaning of Christmas, but never wanted to **accept** the fact that I should receive less and give more until last year.

One day, during the rush of holiday shopping, a young boy, maybe six years old, and his dad came into the grocery store where I worked. While they were standing in line, I overheard the boy tell his father that he wanted to buy his new baby sister a gift for Christmas.

His father quietly replied, "Son, we really can't afford anything more right now. I'm sorry."

Wiping away the tears from his eyes, the boy said, "But Daddy, all I want to do is buy my sister a pacifier and a bib that says, *I love my brother*."

"I'm sorry son, you will have to wait," the father replied.

Continuing to cry, the boy said, "But this is her very first Christmas."

The father, taking the boy's hand, said, "Look, you will have to understand. We cannot afford to buy your little sister anything. We simply don't have the money." The two customers then approached the cash register. Purchasing a small dinner ham, some canned corn and yams, and a pack of rolls for what looked to be a Christmas dinner, the father opened up his torn wallet and pulled out a few food stamps. My heart was broken. I thought about how I felt when my brother and sister were born. They were both so cute and needed someone to take care of them so much. I reached into my pocket, handed the

*I love my brother*

15

boy a five-dollar bill, and winked. His eyes lit up as he turned to his dad and said, "Daddy, now I can buy my sister a Christmas gift?"

His father responded by gently asking him to return the money. After an **exchange** of words, I insisted that the young boy keep the money. I then wished them a Merry Christmas as they left the checkout line and headed to the door.

A little while later, the boy trotted back into the grocery store, his hand tightly gripping a white plastic sack. He pulled out a pink pacifier and a little pink and blue bib that read, "I Love My Brother." He thanked me and held up his arms. Filled with joy, I bent down and gave him a hug.

"Thank you very much!" he said excitedly. He then held out his hand with a dollar bill and some change.

I told the boy to keep the change and buy a gift for himself. He smiled and said, "Come here, I want to show you something," he said. I followed him out of the store and into the parking lot to an old brown truck. Inside were his baby sister and dad. They had brought the baby for me to see. I felt quite honored. The father tied the pink felt bib around her chin and the boy tried to put the pacifier in her mouth. Instead of accepting the pacifier, though, she let out a screeching cry.

"Oops! I should have waited," said the boy.

Before the family left, the father came around the car, shook my hand, and said, "Thank you very, very much. I wish you a Merry Christmas too."

"Thanks," I replied. And as I walked back into the store, I experienced a feeling that I had never felt before. I felt proud and happy, but a little ashamed too. For I had always thought that Christmas was a time to receive gifts. Now I was certain that it was better to give them. Not only did it make others feel better, but it made me feel better too.

# READING CHALLENGE

Name ..............................................

### After reading "Christmas in a Grocery Store," answer the following questions.

1. What is the main idea of the story?


2. Place the events below in sequence as they occur in the story.

_____The two customers then approached the cash register.

_____"Son, we really can't afford anything..."

_____They had brought the baby for me to see.

_____Never wanted to accept the fact that I should receive less...

_____I told the boy to keep the change and buy a gift for himself.

_____For I had always thought that Christmas was a time to receive gifts.

3. What does Christmas mean to you? (If you don't celebrate Christmas, briefly describe another holiday that you celebrate). Use a separate sheet of paper if necessary.


## Finding Details

4. The narrator of this story worked at _____.
5. How much money did the narrator give the boy? _____.
6. The boy wanted to buy his baby sister two items: _____
   and _____.
7. What type of vehicle did the father own? _____.
8. The father purchased what four items at the grocery store? _____.

## Working with Vocabulary

9. What is another word that means the same as <u>exchange</u>?


10. What is an antonym for the word <u>accept</u>?


11. What form of speech are the words <u>quiet</u> and <u>quite</u>?

## Checking Grammar

"I followed him out of the store and into the parking lot to an old brown truck."

12. What is the subject of the sentence above?

13. List the three prepositional phrases in the sentence above.

14. What tense is the verb?

15. How is the pronoun, <u>him</u>, used in the sentence?

*Total Correct*_____

17

RBP

# SCARECROW

He hung there, only half the straw man he used to be, once the poster boy of farm society. He had become the opposite, with only the distant memories of a life he once enjoyed to pass the time and support his current **existence**. He had lived a normal life once enjoying daily conversations with the crows he was there to protect against as he watched the worms make their way through the rows of fresh vegetables. Now these memories served merely to **sustain** him in the patch of dry dirt which he now called home.

With the passing of days, he watched the sun rise and fall and the night come alive and just as quickly run away. He was wise, yet **helpless**, strung limply upon a cross of old planks and broomsticks. Rocks, speckled with dry, crusted mud, formed the foundation on which he hung.

He hung there by himself with an everlasting desire to speak to the birds he once called friends, and to watch the beauty of growth as carrots and onions poked through the fresh earth. He wanted the **freedom** found in the midst of a green field. He wanted the same freedom he enjoyed as a child at play on his post, having no worries, only excitement and adventures each and every day.

Now he wanted to break free from the strings of old twine that bound him, bury the broomstick on which he hung, and scream to the world that he was someone!

# READING CHALLENGE

### After reading "Scarecrow," answer the following questions.

1. "He wanted the freedom found in the midst of a green field." Who is "He" in this sentence?
   A. crow          B. scarecrow          C. society          D. Jim

2. What is the main idea of this story?


## Learning Vocabulary

3. "Now these memories served merely to <u>sustain</u> him in the patch of dry dirt which he now called home." What is another word for <u>sustain</u>?
   A. support          B. diminish          C. mock          D. enjoy

4. In the first paragraph, which word means "<u>the state or fact of having life</u>."
   A. society          B. memories          C. existence          D. effort

5. What is an antonym for <u>freedom</u>?
   A. swallow          B. demolish          C. consume          D. restriction

6. What rhymes with the word <u>thought</u>?
   A. idea          B. bought          C. opinion          D. thinking

7. Look at the word <u>helpless</u> in the second paragraph. The suffix "less" means "without." Given this information, what does the word <u>helpless</u> mean?
   A. weak or dependent                     C. powerful
   B. helpful                               D. independent

## Using Figurative Language

8. Look at the sentence in the third paragraph: "He wanted the freedom found in the midst of a green field." What poetic device is being used in this expression?
   A. simile          B. pun          C. alliteration          D. paradox

9. Read the following sentence: "To watch the beauty of growth as carrots and onions poked through the fresh earth." This sentence is constructed in a way that creates a picture in the reader's mind. What do you call this technique?
   A. alliteration          B. metaphor          C. simile          D. imagery

# Granddad

Today at school my English teacher, Mrs. Brindle, asked everyone in the class to tell a story about a real life hero or heroine. The person could be a stranger or someone close to you, as long as he or she really existed and wasn't a comic book or cartoon character.

One kid told about a close friend who risked his life saving someone from drowning in an icy lake somewhere in Montana. Another kid shared a story about his sister running her first marathon. I chose to tell everyone about my great-grandfather.

My great-grandfather didn't do anything like climb the highest mountain in North America or invent the artificial heart. There was no one special deed that made my great-grandfather a hero. No, he was a hero because of the way he lived his life, day after day, month after month, and year after year.

Granddad, which is how I always referred to him, was born the oldest son to a family of eight living in San Francisco. During his life, he encountered many hardships, including the Great San Francisco Earthquake and the Great Depression. But probably the most difficult thing he experienced was being abandoned by his father when he was just eleven years old. To this day, he doesn't know why his father left his family, because his father was never heard from again. At the time, Granddad was deeply hurt. But he says that when he looks back now, he realizes that the experience helped make him who he is today.

Being the oldest son, my great-grandfather felt financially responsible for his mom and family. Hearing the news about his father leaving, a friend who owned a convenience store down the street offered Granddad a job. He couldn't go to school and work at the same time, so he was forced to drop out. He never completed high school, let alone graduate from college. But he learned a lot about accounting, and managing a store, and was given a real lesson in "personal responsibility," as he calls it.

After five years of work at the general store, he was offered a sales job with a **haggard**, old mining-supply company in Nevada. He worked hard for years and saved as much money as he could while sending half of his salary home to his family. The company started doing really well, due, in part, to Granddad's hard work. It wasn't long before he started building up a savings which he eventually used to purchase a home for his own wife and children.

By the time Granddad retired, he had amassed a small fortune, which he left to his children and grandchildren. He accomplished all this through sheer perseverance and hard work. My great-grandfather stands to prove that heroes are all around us doing heroic things every day.

# READING CHALLENGE

### After reading " Granddad," answer the following questions.

1. What does the word <u>haggard</u> mean?


2. Granddad moved to _____ to take a job at a mining-supply company?
   A. New York
   B. San Francisco
   C. Nevada
   D. Atlanta


3. How old was Granddad when his father abandoned him?


4. What was not one of the lessons Granddad learned working at the convenience store?
   A. a lesson in accounting
   B. a lesson in managing a store
   C. a lesson in "personal responsibility"
   D. a lesson in using the cash register


5. In the space below, write a short paragraph about a real life hero or heroine in your life. This person can be someone from your own family, a friend, or even someone that you have never met personally.

Remember, if you don't know what a word means, look it up in a dictionary! You'll do better in the exercises!

RBP

# AN ODE TO A POND

Once I sat in my little boat
in a still pond I sat afloat.
I saw the sun slip from the sky
and knew that evening was a nigh.

But when I took my oar to stroke,
I heard the frogs begin to croak.
And then the night began to fill
with <u>mystic</u> songs as I sat still.

The songs were about times of past
and memories that would last and last.
But then I heard a song so sad
by a little frog upon a lily pad.

The song was all about his bride,
who left, broke his heart and hurt his pride.
And oh that pond became a sea
of sorrow as he sang to me.

Later the pond was silence filled,
and the air became so very still.
I spotted a doe with her fawn,
and then I saw the start of <u>dawn</u>.

## READING CHALLENGE

After reading "An Ode To A Pond," answer the following questions.

1. The setting of this poem is a
   A. boat.        B. pond.        C. lily pad.        D. beach.

2. "And then the night began to fill/with <u>mystic</u> songs as I sat still." Choose a word that means the same as the underlined word.
   A. magical        B. happy        C. sad        D. loud

3. "I spotted a doe with her fawn/and then I saw the start of dawn." The word <u>dawn</u> means <u>sunrise</u>. In the context of the poem, what else could the word mean?
   A. brightness        C. beginning
   B. darkness        D. happiness

**Total Correct** _____

# Reflections on Pinewood Lake

Journal: June 12, 1999

I have waited all year for summer to get here. Camp is incredible fun! The towering mountains in the woods of North Carolina are like majestic spires on a cathedral. And the lake, **nestled** at the base of the mountains, is cool and tranquil.

Don't get me wrong. School was great fun this year. There are many places here where I can get away and read for a spell. Last summer I found a spot that no one knows about, not even my best friend Alana, who has come back this summer. Last summer I read *Bridge to Teriabithia* in my secluded spot. I loved the book, even though it was a little sad.

Journal: June 14, 1999

Yesterday, Julie, Ted and I went canoeing on the lake. The lake becomes more beautiful every year. One part of the lake stretches quite a distance into a narrow cove, which has trees and vines that hang out over the water. We took our time and listened carefully as we quietly paddled up the cove. Julie and Ted are fun to travel with because they enjoy the outdoors as much as I do. Also, they believe, as I, in protecting and **maintaining** our forests.

Once I saw a duck with five ducklings swimming proudly behind.

I would love to be a bird for one day. To experience the freedom of flight would be fantastic. Also, I saw two beavers sawing a log. Maybe they were preparing a home for winter or simply repairing an existing home. I almost forgot. I also heard some turkeys. I know they were turkeys because I recognize their call from having heard and seen them last summer.

Journal: June 17, 1999

I forgot to write in my journal yesterday. When Lisa, my counselor, first assigned journal writing, I was a bit aggravated. But now I'm quite used to it. I am making a lot of discoveries about the camp and myself, and writing about them helps to clarify and make sense of it all.

For example: I'm a little worried about Julie. Her mother called today and told her that her brother had been taken to the hospital. Julie wouldn't tell me all the details, but she did say that her mother promised everything would be okay. I hope her mother is right. I don't know if Julie is embarrassed about her brother and the reasons behind his having to go to the hospital, but I wish she felt comfortable sharing them with me. There is really nothing she could ever say that would change my opinion about her. She will always be my dear friend.

Name

 **READING CHALLENGE**

### After reading "Reflections on Pinewood Lake," answer the following questions.

## Finding Details

**1. Pinewood Lake is located in**
   A. Alabama.      B. Mississippi.      C. North Carolina.      D. Oregon.

**2. The writer has just completed what grade?**
   A. fifth      B. does not say      C. seventh      D. eighth

**3. Who is the writer's "best" friend?**
   A. Alana      B. Julie      C. Ted      D. Lisa

**4. The writer saw two of these animals preparing a home.**
   A. turkeys      B. ducks      C. squirrels      D. beavers

**5. Julie's brother was admitted to**
   A. law school.      C. a hospital.
   B. a drug rehabilitation center.      D. a mental rehabilitation center.

**6. With whom did the writer go canoeing?**
   A. Lisa and Ted      C. Ted and Alana
   B. Ted and Julie      D. Alana and Julie

## Working with Vocabulary

**7. What rhymes with the word <u>nestled?</u>**
   A. wrestled      B. cuddled      C. situated      D. located

**8. What is a synonym for the word <u>maintaining?</u>**
   A. sustaining      B. recovering      C. cleaning      D. menacing

## Using Language

**9. What kind of mood is reflected in the first paragraph of the first journal entry?**
   A. angry      B. sad      C. remorseful      D. serene

**10. What is the simile in the first paragraph?**
   A. for this summer      C. in the woods
   B. like majestic spires      D. so much fun

*Total Correct*_____

# Lady of the Harbor

Just beyond the crowded streets,
she stands tall and brave,
bathed in robes of green,
her hand lifted high above the **harbor**.
Though she says nothing,
she speaks a thousand words of freedom.

# READING CHALLENGE

After reading "Lady of the Harbor," answer the following questions.

1. In the poem, who is the "lady?"

2. What is the "lady" wearing?

3. In your own words, what do you think the "Lady of the Harbor" is saying in the last sentence of the poem?  Who is she saying this to?

4. The word <u>harbor</u> in this poem means
   A.  an inlet for anchoring ships.
   B.  a restaurant.
   C.  a garage.
   D.  an area between two islands.

## Writing to Think

5. Create an image or short poem in which you use personification (a writing technique in which an inanimate object is given human-like characteristics).

Total Correct_____

# The Scare in the Mountains

**I** felt a chill as my dad and I made our way up the east ridge of Lonely Mountain. It was the middle of October, but the air was unseasonably cold. I looked up at the sky to see that the clouds had grown **ominous** and gray. "Looks like a storm is coming," I said to Dad.

"You're right, but I think we can make it to the top and down again before dark," he said. We continued on. Neither of us said anything for a while. Intent on reaching our goal, we focused all our energy on moving as quickly and steadily as possible. All that distracted me was my back, which ached underneath the weight of my pack.

When we were just 300 feet from the top, we heard a loud crack, and seconds later, saw a flash of lightning not far from where we stood. We stopped and my dad had turned towards me as if to say something when I noticed his hair was standing on end like a porcupine's. I started to laugh, and pointed at him. Gingerly, he put his hand to his head and felt the hair, which elicited an immediate reaction.

"Run!" he yelled, motioning for me to turn back down the ridge. It started to rain, and run we did. We ran over rocks, we ran through grass, we ran through the rain and ducked under trees, and jumped across streams until we came to a cave where we had enjoyed lunch earlier.

"Inside," said my dad, his voice almost inaudible against the wind and rain of the storm. Once inside, we caught our breath and waited for the storm to abate before heading back out to return home. While we waited, my dad explained that it wasn't the rain we were running from, but the lightning which, at high altitudes, can be very dangerous. He said his hair standing on end was a sign of electricity, which meant that lightning was near and could have hit us had we stayed exposed on the ridge for much longer. My face must have looked stricken with fear, because my dad looked at me **empathetically** and explained that we were safe for the time being.

"If I had not known there was a cave nearby, we wouldn't have tried to beat the storm to the top. During a thunderstorm, on top of a mountain is the last place you want to be," he said. "We're okay now. There's nothing to worry about inside this cave."

Trusting my dad to see us safely to the bottom, I smiled. He was the best!

# READING CHALLENGE

### After reading "The Scare in the Mountains," answer the following questions.

1. **How many feet from the top were the hikers before they were forced to turn back?**
   A. 300      B. 600      C. 330      D. 900

2. **To look at someone <u>empathetically</u> is to**
   A. look with disgust
   B. look with extreme sympathy
   C. look with dismay
   D. look with dissatisfaction

3. **The boy compares his father's hair standing on end to a**
   A. prickly pear.      B. fuzzy peach.      C. porcupine.      D. static electricity.

4. **In this story, <u>ominous</u> means**
   A. fluffy.      B. white.      C. scattered.      D. threatening.

5. **This story takes place in**
   A. October.      B. September.      C. November.      D. December.

6. **The boy and his dad were in the mountains**
   A. to find a cave.
   B. to pick berries.
   C. on a hunting trip.
   D. on a hike.

Remember, if you don't know what a word means, look it up in a dictionary! You'll do better in the exercises!

**Total Correct**_____

RBP

# A Dream

Walking barefoot through the tall grass in my backyard, I grew contemplative and listless. I sat down to think about life when, before I knew it, I fell asleep and drifted off to another world...

Suddenly, I was sitting somewhere outside, a cool breeze flowing through my long hair, when out of nowhere a little girl named Nancy grabbed my hand and said, "Come on, my friend. We need to go."

Nancy looked like she was only about six years old, but she had the strength of a soldier, the wisdom of a queen, and the charisma of a movie star. As we walked, she talked of peace and love for the entire world. Not the typical conversation you get with a six-year-old!

We wandered into a beautiful flower garden. It was incredible, like nothing I had ever seen before! Every color of the rainbow was visible. The reds, yellows and blues were so vibrant and rich! No artist would ever be capable of painting this picture!

"Smell that beautiful, sweet smell and feel the warm sunshine," said Nancy. **Spellbound**, I watched her pick the prettiest flower in the garden. As she did, she looked at me and said, "What does this pretty flower mean to you?" But before I could answer, I awoke....

It was all a dream, but since that afternoon in the garden, whenever I see a beautiful flower, I think of Nancy, and all the wonderful things she taught me.

# READING CHALLENGE

### After reading "A Dream," answer the following questions.

1. **The story is mainly about**
   A. the strength of a soldier.
   B. red and yellow flowers.
   C. thinking and reflecting about life.
   D. weeping willows.

2. **Someone who is <u>spellbound</u> is**
   A. determined.    B. entranced.    C. a poor speller.    D. angry.

3. **Nancy is**
   A. the beautiful flower.
   B. the speaker's sister.
   C. the gardener.
   D. the girl in the dream.

4. **"She had the strength of a soldier." What figure of speech is used?**
   A. metaphor
   B. simile
   C. personification
   D. pun

# The Calf

One day, about a year ago, I ventured out from the confines of my four-cornered room and headed for some woods and farmland near my house. I needed to get away and think.

Though it was early in the fall, the leaves had already begun to gather on the ground. As I walked, my mind and thoughts became **preoccupied** with everything around me instead of my personal problems, which had dogged me all day. The whispers of the wind and the leaves crunching beneath my feet overwhelmed my senses, drowning all my worries. I touched a few of the trees and rocks to reassure myself that they were real, because everything seemed so **surreal**.

I sallied forth in this state of mind until I came upon a mother cow and her newborn calf. The calf made funny, almost human, noises as it blindly wobbled back and forth beneath its mother. It sounded a lot like my little sister when she was a baby. It was always my understanding that calves were born in the springtime. But I was surprised and delighted by the vision before me, and I stopped to watch the two interact.

Truly, September is a colorful time in Tennessee. Fall typically makes me nostalgic. But seeing the cow and its newborn calf filled me with hope for the future instead of a desire to revisit the past.

Whatever problems I had that day disappeared as I stood there in the pasture that afternoon. I stayed there for quite a while, watching the sun until it descended behind the hills, its warm, pink glow filling the skies with radiant color.

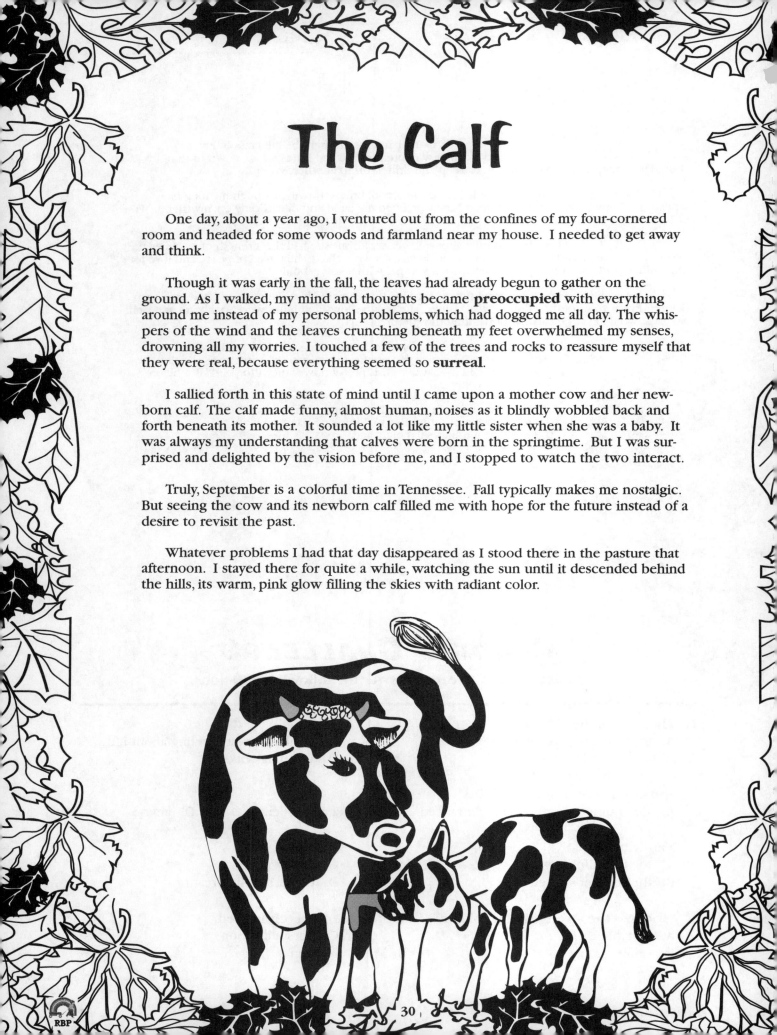

# READING CHALLENGE

### After reading "The Calf," answer the following questions.

1. **The speaker may be described as**
   A. someone who thinks about life.
   B. someone who tries anything.
   C. a good student at school.
   D. someone who doesn't care.

2. **The setting of the story is**
   A. October in a pasture in Tennessee.
   B. September in Alabama farmland.
   C. September in a pasture in Tennessee.
   D. September in the mountains of Utah.

3. **The simile in the story is**
   A. like a cow bellowing.
   B. like a dogwood tree dying.
   C. a mother cow looking.
   D. like my little sister.

4. **What is another word for <u>preoccupied</u>?**
   A. settled          B. engrossed          C. satisfied          D. safe

5. **The speaker leaves the house to**
   A. look for the cow.
   B. work in the pasture.
   C. get away and think.
   D. go to school.

6. **The word <u>surreal</u> means**
   A. real.          B. dreamlike.          C. beautiful.          D. colorful.

7. **Which happens first?**

A. _____ "...its warm, pink glow filling the skies with radiant color."

B. _____ "The calf made funny, almost human, noises... ."

C. _____ "...the leaves crunching beneath my feet overwhelmed my senses, drowning all my worries."

D. _____ "I ventured out from the confines of my four-cornered room... ."

8. **After having spent the day in the woods and farmlands, the speaker**
   A. realizes his/her problems can be worked out.
   B. becomes depressed.
   C. decides to skip school the next week.
   D. plans to speak with his dad about his problems.

RBP

# TIGER TOWN

Yesterday, I read a story in the newspaper about a place in Montana called Tiger Town. Tiger Town is an animal sanctuary and rescue facility for large cats like tigers, lions, leopards, pumas and jaguars. A sanctuary is a lot like a shelter for dogs or house cats, except it's permanent.

The reason these sanctuaries are necessary is because there are, surprisingly, a lot of homeless large cats. It's hard to imagine a homeless tiger. But they're homeless because many states have no licensing requirements or regulations for the purchase and keeping of these great cats. Too many people buy a tiger when it is a cub and relatively harmless, only to find out later that they have a wild animal, not a pet, on their hands. Experts will tell you that there is simply no way to make a house pet out of a tiger, a lion, or any other big cat. However, most owners of large cats do not discover this until it's too late.

For this and other reasons, big cats often find themselves without a home, and they must be placed somewhere or be destroyed. There are very few options available to those with unwanted cats, and a sanctuary is the most **humane**. Sanctuaries never sell the animals they house, nor breed them. They are safe places where the inhabitants are fed a proper diet and given medical attention and wide-open spaces to relax and be content for as long as they live.

Because of a lack of funding and trained personnel, there are very few of these sanctuaries in the United States. It is estimated that there are over 5,000 big cats in private ownership across the country. As more states pass legislation to ban possession of the big cats, the need for sanctuaries grows.

The sanctuary in Montana takes donations from people who are interested in helping the cats. So I've decided to send in some of the money I've accumulated in my savings account. I want to help any way that I can!

# READING CHALLENGE

### After reading "Tiger Town," answer the following questions.

1. **Tiger Town is located in**
   A. southern Oregon.
   B. Montana.
   C. northern Utah.
   D. Las Vegas.

2. **The story is mainly about**
   A. what great pets tigers make.
   B. the slow extinction of tigers.
   C. the importance of animal sanctuaries.
   D. saving your money.

3. **To pass legislation is to**
   A. enact a law.
   B. convict a criminal.
   C. take away someone's license.
   D. punish tiger owners.

4. **How many cats are estimated to be in private ownership across the country?**
   A. 500     B. 3     C. 6000     D. 5000

5. **A synonym for <u>humane</u> is**
   A. clean.     B. compassionate.     C. orderly.     D. professional.

6. **What makes an animal sanctuary different from an animal shelter?**
   A. it's larger
   B. it's temporary
   C. it's permanent
   D. it's not different

7. **Which of the following is not the kind of cat housed at an animal sanctuary?**
   A. Siamese     B. tiger     C. leopard     D. puma

8. **The sanctuaries need donations because**
   A. they lack funding and trained personnel.
   B. they don't spend their money wisely.
   C. large cats like to receive gifts.
   D. they don't need donations.

Remember, if you don't know what a word means, look it up in a dictionary! You'll do better in the exercises!

RBP

# Boom Boom's Turkey Farm

Yesterday I went to my grandparents' house and had a fantastic time. Actually, I always have a fantastic time when I visit, but yesterday was the best by far! When I arrived, I found a raccoon's nest. It wasn't that big, about the size of a beach ball. What made it really neat was that there were two baby raccoons playing inside. I watched them for a little while, but not too long. I didn't want momma raccoon coming back from dinner to find an uninvited guest sitting in her living room!

I ran in the house to tell grampa of my big discovery. He was sure to have a funny story about a raccoon, he's a comedian. That's what makes it so fun to talk with him. Okay, he is not a real comedian, but he sure acts like one!

When I got in the house I found grampa waltzing around the kitchen like a king. Suddenly, the phone rang. "Quiet, quiet everybody," he whispered. "I've been waiting for this phone call all day, it's an important one." Grampa has a good sense of humor, he's always telling jokes, laughing and having a good time. He smiled and gave me a wink as he picked up the phone. In his most serious voice he said, "Boom Boom's Turkey Farm, how may I help you." My sister and I howled so hard our sides hurt. Grampa doesn't own a turkey farm.

He delivers fish!

Grampa is old. I think fifty or sixty. He says he still feels like a young man though, and he still plays with me and all my friends from school like he is our age. He even beat Billy Basham in a race around the house last summer, and Billy is the fastest runner in school! If any of my friends are ever in a bad mood or just want to talk they will stop by at grampa's because they know he will cheer them up. I spend a lot of time talking with him too. We actually take turns talking and listening. I can sit for hours listening to stories that don't seem to have a point, but at the end there will always be a lesson. Like, work hard and do your best, but never forget to laugh!

My grandfather is a wonderful, likable, funny human being who enjoys life to the fullest and helps everybody around him enjoy theirs to the fullest too. If you are ever lucky enough to meet him, ask him to tell you a funny story. Like the one about the two baby raccoons and their mother who was the size of a horse!

Okay, are you ready to learn my grampa's real name? It's even funnier than he is! Belar Goodwin. Can you believe it? I think grampa's mother was a comedian too! I wonder if she lived on a turkey farm?

Boom Boom's Turkey Farm

# READING CHALLENGE

## After reading "Boom Boom's Turkey Farm," answer the following questions.

1. What is the main idea of the story?

2. Discuss what one of your grandfathers means to you. Use a separate sheet of paper.

3. Place the events below in sequence as they occur in the story.

_____I spend a lot of time talking with him too.

_____I found Grampa waltzing around the kitchen like a king.

_____Yesterday, I went to my grandparent's house... .

_____I wonder if she lived on a turkey farm?

_____Like the one about the two baby raccoons...

_____In his most serious voice he said, "Boom Boom's Turkey Farm..."

4. **Boom Boom's Turkey Farm is**
   A. Grandfather's turkey farm.
   B. the farm next door.
   C. Grandfather's telephone response.
   D. the speakers' farm.

5. **How does the speaker feel about his grandfather?**
   A. he talks too much
   B. he's not serious enough in front of the speaker's friends
   C. he's a good fisherman
   D. he's a great friend with a good sense of humor

## Finding Details

6. How old is the speaker's grandfather?

7. What job does Grampa have?

8. Who is the fastest runner in school?

9. What is Grampa's real name?

## Checking Grammar

"Grampa has a good sense of humor, he's always telling jokes, laughing and having a good time."

10. What is the subject in the sentence above?

11. What is the verb in the sentence above?

# Mom at Bat

Our town's Goodtimes Festival fell on a humid Saturday morning in July this year. I clearly remember the days leading up to it, because I wanted them to last forever. To my **chagrin**, and the shame of my brother, Mom was going to compete in the annual softball tournament this year.

But the day did finally arrive and my mother, brother and I made our way to the ball-park. By the time we arrived, most of the crowd was already seated, talking excitedly and gearing up for a fun-filled day. My brother and I took our seats in the stands, while our mom strutted gallantly onto the field.

She joined her team, all dressed head-to-toe in blue and heading for the dugouts. The umpires took their places on the field as one of them roared, "Let's play ball. Batter up!" And the crowd, which had been cheering, fell silent. The first batter on the opposing, white-shirted team took her stance. And my brother and I watched patiently as she, and the two following batters, struck out.

The first batter of my unathletic mom's team was up next. I watched her strike out, pondering over the reasons my mother was so intent on putting me through this embarrassment. The second batter was no better than the first, swinging the bat as if she were swatting flies. My Mom was up next and I was **skeptical**. I could feel my face turn red and I looked about timidly hoping no one would notice whose child I was.

The pitcher wound up and I winced as the ball flew past my mom like a rocket. I don't think she even caught a glimpse of it. "Strike one," yelled the umpire as the catcher returned the ball to the pitcher. I watched as my mom warmed up for the next pitch, swinging the bat around like a helicopter.

I swallowed hard, but it was if an enormous grape was lodged somewhere in my throat. The pitcher released the second pitch and a look of terror grew on the spectators' faces as my mother

swung and missed the ball again. "Strike two!" yelled the umpire.

Mom took a step back from the plate and peered at me. She looked like she needed encouragement, but all I could muster was a shrug of the shoulders and roll of the eyes. But this seemed to have worked, because she stepped up to the plate, and readied herself like a professional ballplayer who had a date with a home run. Dust stirred where she stood, eyes trained on the pitcher's mound, anxious for the pitch.

By this time I was feeling **nauseous** and likely to faint. I considered sneaking out the back gate to the car, but I knew everyone would notice me, including my mom. I sank lower into my seat. With one eye open, I watched the pitcher wind up and throw one doozy of a fastball. Everything appeared like it was in slow motion. The ball, spinning, got closer and closer and closer, and then I heard a "whack!" I opened my other eye out of disbelief and still couldn't accept what I was witnessing — my mom running as fast as her legs would allow from first to second base, second to third and, finally, third to home. When she reached home, my brother and I stood up with the crowd and cheered. Seeing us standing, my mom smiled and gave us the thumb's up. In acknowledgment of her victory, we did the same.

That afternoon, I learned something about my mom that I had never considered before. She didn't let her fear of failure or embarrassment stand in the way of trying something new or having a good time. "Maybe she is cool after all," I thought to myself, watching the remainder of the game with pride.

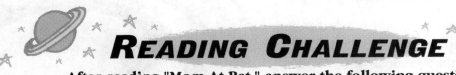

# READING CHALLENGE

After reading "Mom At Bat," answer the following questions.

1. **The story is mainly about**
   A. playing baseball once a year.
   B. feeling sick at ball games.
   C. learning to accept one's parents.
   D. what to do on a Saturday.

2. **What is the simile in the sentence: "The second batter was no better than the first, swinging the bat as if she were swatting flies."**
   A. no better than
   B. swinging the bat
   C. the second batter
   D. as if she were swatting flies

3. **The word <u>nauseous</u> means**
   A. happy.       B. sick.       C. overweight.       D. angry.

4. **Why is there a baseball game on this Saturday morning?**
   A. there is a baseball game every Saturday
   B. the game is part of an annual festival
   C. the two teams had planned the game weeks ago
   D. the game was organized to raise money

5. **What is another word for <u>skeptical</u>?**
   A. doubtful       B. wishful       C. excited       D. concerned

6. **The speaker in the story wanted to sneak out the back gate to the car because**
   A. the speaker feared being seen by a friend.
   B. the speaker was embarrassed for Mom.
   C. the speaker had the flu.
   D. the speaker had forgotten something.

7. **The speaker's mom plays with the**
   A. blue team.
   B. purple team.
   C. yellow team.
   D. green team.

8. **Before the speaker's mom hits the home run, she**
   A. gives the crowd the thumb's up.
   B. winks at the crowd.
   C. telephones her husband at work.
   D. readies herself like a professional.

9. **"To my <u>chagrin</u>, and the shame of my brother, Mom was going to compete in the annual softball tournament this year." What does the word <u>chagrin</u> mean in the above sentence?**
   A. annoyance       B. embarrassment       C. delight       D. regret

38          *Total Correct*_____

# THE GAME

One minute left, down by ten,
The coach says to me, "You're going in."
With four personal fouls and one to give
I say to myself, "How will I live?"

As I rise from the hard, uncomfortable chair,
I check my uniform and fix my hair.
I walk toward the spot where I check in,
see my girl in the crowd, and give her a grin.

The ref's whistle screams, the horn blows.
I walk on the court and hear the crowd go, "uh-oh!"
Five straight times someone passes the ball,
I shoot it — SWISH — it was nothing at all.

I shoot for the final time. The score is now tied.
The ref calls a foul, and I go to the line.
Taking a deep breath and looking at the goal,
I shoot the ball and get the lucky roll.

The contest is over. We won the game.
Without question, I am inducted into the Hall of Fame.
Tim Duncan and the San Antonio Spurs, take heed,
Tonight's game was just chicken feed.

# READING CHALLENGE

### After reading "The Game," answer the following questions.

1. **Who does the speaker see in the crowd?**
   A. his coach
   B. Tim Duncan
   C. his girlfriend
   D. his mom

2. **What is the game?**
   A. baseball
   B. basketball
   C. soccer
   D. football

3. **In line 14, "The ref calls a foul, and I go to the line," what is "the line"?**
   A. an out-of-bounds line
   C. the line of scrimmage
   B. the fifty-yard line
   D. the free-throw line

# An Essay On The Grand Canyon

The Grand Canyon is one of the natural wonders of the world. It is over 2 billion years old and is located in northern Arizona. The entire Grand Canyon National Park encompasses 277 miles of the Colorado River and adjacent lands. The canyon itself is one of the most spectacular examples of water erosion in the world, and is visited by more than five million people every year!

Though you can get a great view of the canyon from the rim, the best way to appreciate the area is to hike into it. You have to be prepared to handle extreme variations in temperature and weather, so you must carry plenty of water. The reason for the temperature variation is that the South and North Rims are 7,000 and 8,000 feet above sea level! The canyon is roughly one mile deep, which means that even though it can snow on the top rim in the winter and get cool during the summer, the canyon stays quite warm down inside. In fact, the average difference in temperature from the bottom to the top of the canyon is 25 degrees! Summer temperatures along the Colorado River at the canyon bottom can reach 120 degrees Fahrenheit. This is another reason why you need to bring a lot of water!

For people in good physical condition, the hike from the rim down to the river at the canyon's bottom can be accomplished in a day. But once you're inside, you'll want to spend at least a week exploring. There are so many cool things to see!

Several desert animals make their home in the canyon, including lizards, bats, ring-tailed cats, frogs, mice, fish, and an endless number of birds. Plant life consists mostly of cactus and low lying bushes, but a few trees grow at the water's edge.

The Colorado River is amazing! It is one of the North American continent's largest rivers and if you stick around long enough, you will probably even see a team of white water rafters float by. You can swim in the water to cool off after your long hike down, but because it comes from a large dam, the water is extremely cold. You must also be careful of its swift current, which can be very deceiving. Personally, I like to lie on my back late into the evening and just stare at the stars. I can do this for hours!

Ultimately, it doesn't matter if you hike, raft or look at the canyon from above. Because no matter how one encounters the canyon, it's a "grand" experience!

# READING CHALLENGE

### After reading "An Essay On The Grand Canyon," answer the following questions.

1. **What is the main idea of this essay?**


2. **What's the benefit of hiking into the canyon according to the essay?**


3. **Place the sentences below in the sequence they occur in the essay.**

_____ . . . its a "grand" experience!

_____ The canyon is roughly one mile deep. . .

_____ Personally, I like to lie on my back late into the evening. . .

_____ The entire Grand Canyon National Park encompasses 277 miles of the Colorado River. . .

_____ Summer temperatures along the Colorado River. . .

_____ and is visited by more than five million people every year!

4. **How hot can the bottom of the canyon get in the summer?**
   A. 100 degrees Fahrenheit
   B. 110 degrees Fahrenheit
   C. 120 degrees Fahrenheit
   D. 120 degrees Celsius

5. **What do you "suppose" was the primary cause of the canyon's erosion?**
   A. lightning     B. the sun     C. the wind     D. the river

## Finding Details

6. **How many feet high is the North Rim?**


7. **Why is the water of the Colorado River so cold?**


8. **Where is the Grand Canyon located?**


9. **How long should it take someone in good physical condition to hike from the rim of the canyon to the bottom?**


10. **Do you want to visit the Grand Canyon? Why or why not?**

# Help! I'm Lost

On December 24, 1988, my little brother Christopher was born into the world. The event was one of happiness, joy, and total frustration for many, including me. I was in the eighth grade at Swanee Middle, and school was out for Christmas vacation.

The day after Christopher was born my granny, my cousin Mark, and I went to the hospital to see my mom and little Christopher. We were all so excited about seeing my little brother that we didn't have dinner before we left. After visiting Mom and Christopher for a short while, we decided to eat something in the hospital cafeteria before we left to go home. Mark was famished, he said, whenever I saw him eat he always ate like a horse.

None of us knew where the cafeteria was, and the hospital had twenty-six floors. "Let's ask a nurse," said Mark.

"Excuse me, Miss, where is the cafeteria?" asked Granny, when we finally found a nurse.

"On the third floor," replied the nurse.

We hurried into the elevator and went to the third floor. Looking around, we found no cafeteria, so Granny asked a second nurse about the cafeteria.

"Seventh floor," the second nurse responded. Once again, we hopped into the elevator and stopped at the seventh floor. However, looking around, we discovered there was no cafeteria on this floor. What was going on? Why were we being given the runaround by the nurses? All three of us were beginning to feel somewhat paranoid and insignificant.

"Granny, I am hungry," I said hesitatingly.

"I know, Honey, and so are Mark and I," she told me. Again, Granny stopped a nurse and asked the same question for the third time.

"Fourteenth floor," the third nurse said very politely.

As we stepped out of the elevator, we noticed a sign down the hall that read "Welcome to the Children's Hospital." Along the hall and on the walls and floors were painted animals and toys of many different colors and shapes.

Each of us turned and looked at the other.

It didn't take us very many more minutes to realize that the hospital was actually two hospitals in one building. The first thirteen floors were St. Luke's Hospital, and the last thirteen floors were the Children's Hospital. "Let's look around anyway. It might actually be on this floor," I finally said. I was wrong; it wasn't. Tired and frustrated, we took the elevator to the main floor and walked across the street to have dinner at a sandwich deli.

**Hospital Cafeteria**

# READING CHALLENGE

### After reading "Help! I'm Lost," answer the following questions.

1. **A word that means the same as insignificant is**
   A. unimportant.  B. happy.  C. important.  D. irrelevant.

2. **The three people visiting the hospital were**
   A. Granny, Mark, Christopher.  B. Mark, Granny, Mom. mom
   C. Mark, Granny, speaker.  D. speaker, Granny, Christopher.

3. **Which one of the following events happened first?**
   A. As we stepped out of the elevator, we noticed a sign down the hall.
   B. We decided to eat something in the hospital cafeteria.
   C. Tired and frustrated, we took the elevator to the basement.
   D. Looking around, we found no cafeteria.

4. **"Mark was famished, he said, but he always ate like a horse whenever I saw him eat."**
   **Context clues which might suggest the meaning of the word famished is**
   A. whenever I saw.  B. ate like a horse.
   C. he said.  D. but he always.

5. **Why did the speaker visit the hospital?**
   A. to visit Granny who had recently been hospitalized due to an illness
   B. to visit Mark who had knee surgery because of an injury
   C. to visit Mom who had been hospitalized because of the flu
   D. to visit Mom who had had a baby boy, the speaker's brother

6. **The speaker said once that Mark "ate like a horse." The literary or writing technique is called**
   A. metaphor.  B. simile.  C. pun.  D. personification.

7. **Other than the sign that read, "Welcome to the Children's Hospital," what might be another clue that the speaker is in the Children's Hospital?**
   A. The nurse told them that this was the Children's Hospital.
   B. The two doctors on the elevator told them.
   C. There were animals and toys painted on the walls and floors.
   D. The loudspeaker on the elevator announced the location.

# T H E

It was dark and cold on the **tundra**. Alexis and Marty, who had been running their sleds through the night, decided it was time to rest. Alexis was training for the big sled race next month. She stopped near a clearing in the middle of a patch of trees. Marty, her husband, slowed his team of dogs and rested with her.

Five years ago, Marty had won the race Alexis was now preparing for. This year he had decided against entering the competition in order to manage the support crew for his wife and her team of dogs. Marty and Alexis were very competitive with one another, and Marty had to use all his restraint to keep from quitting on Alexis. After all, there was a chance he could win again and return the next year as the reigning champion. But Alexis had been there to manage his support crew and watch him as he crossed the finish line last year. Being there for her was the least he could do, he reasoned. Besides, Marty would never let Alexis train alone in the wild, and he knew that her mind was set on winning this race. Moreover, he enjoyed their weekend training sessions together and he really wanted to support her.

During the week Marty and Alexis operated their store, which sold outdoor and hiking equipment. All of the residents in their small town shopped there, because of the couple's extensive knowledge and experience with outdoor equipment. The two generally carried equipment with them during their training sessions, as this allowed them to test products and decide whether or not to carry them in the store. This weekend was no different.

After resting for a while, Alexis realized how tired she and her team of dogs were. She brought the subject up with Marty, who agreed that since they were prepared with all the requisite overnight equipment, they should enjoy the evening air and spend the night on the tundra. They set up camp, cooked and ate dinner. Later, they shared opinions with one another about the week's events before climbing into their sleeping bags and falling into a deep, satisfying slumber.

When Marty and Alexis awoke the following morning, they found their tent nearly covered with snow. This delayed their intent to get the camp packed before sunrise. Several hours later, the equipment was packed and the team prepared for the trip home. The snow was deep and powdery — not the best conditions for dogsledding, but that didn't stop Marty and Alexis.

At first everything was going fine, but after three or four hours of traveling, the worst happened. Marty had been in the lead and Alexis was about fifty feet behind when, without warning, the snow collapsed under Marty and his entire team. He, his sled and team of dogs fell about twenty feet into a deep fissure in the icy ground that had been covered and hidden by the newly fallen snow.

Alexis saw Marty fall, and immediately feared for her husband's life. She knew that snow **crevasses** could be endless, and

that no matter how shallow the crevasse might be, Marty had no way of extracting himself from it. As she neared the crevasse, she heard Marty hollering for her. A good sign, she thought, because this meant he probably hadn't been injured too badly, nor had he fallen too far down. She slowed the team to a stop, jumped from her sled and ran to peak over the edge of the crevasse. There was Marty, securely lodged between the ice walls of the crevasse, barely visible. She called to him, and told him to remain calm and relaxed, and that she was going for help.

Alexis was well aware that a rescue of this magnitude couldn't be accomplished alone, and the nearest town was at least five miles away. Marty sounded like he was in pain, and Alexis was concerned she might not make it back in time to administer any necessary first-aid. The sooner she left the better, she thought. So she took off and struck out for the town. She rode faster and harder than ever before. Her team was exhausted from sludging through inches of powder, but she drove them harder. And they responded, carrying her to town in record time! Once in town, she quickly notified the sheriff and rescue squad about what had happened to her husband.

The rescue squad marshalled a group of medical technicians, snowmobiles, and rescue equipment together in good time. Alexis was given a snowmobile so she could lead the team back to Marty, and they were off. Musing upon the squad's swift response, her hopes were raised.

Alexis easily located the crevasse, and led the rescue squad right to Marty. He was still conscious, but very cold from being immobile for so long. After what seemed like hours, the team pulled Marty out of the crevasse, loaded him onto a sick sled and administered some prelimi-

nary first-aid to ready him for the short journey home. Marty was going to be okay, thought Alexis as she trailed the sick sled.

When Marty recovered from the sprained wrist, cuts, bumps and bruises he suffered during the fall, he returned to preparing Alexis for the race. Feeling slightly responsible for her husband's accident, Alexis suggested that Marty run the race instead. Her heart wasn't really in it anymore, and she knew Marty wanted to return and try again for first place. But Marty convinced her that the accident wasn't her fault. "I want to see you win this race," he said. "If you don't try, the accident and all our hard work will have been for nothing."

Alexis finally agreed with Marty and it wasn't long before race day was upon them. At the starting gate, Marty gave Alexis a wink and a smile that helped carry her over the challenging terrain and rigorous course to finish first. When she received the award and was asked to make a speech, she thanked Marty for all his help, strength and emotional support, then handed him the trophy. "This trophy is as much his as mine," she said to the crowd. "We are partners in everything we do."

# READING CHALLENGE

### After reading "The Race," answer the following questions.

1. **The story is mainly about**
   A. competition and cooperation.
   B. competition and jealousy.
   C. surviving during a snowstorm.
   D. winning and cold weather.

2. **A <u>crevasse</u> is a**
   A. pond.  B. well.  C. crack.  D. cave.

3. **The story suggests that**
   A. we should not give up regardless of the obstacles we encounter.
   B. one should never travel after a big snowstorm.
   C. husbands and wives should not compete against one another.
   D. one should always be prepared for cold weather.

4. **A <u>tundra</u> is**
   A. a high mountain in Greenland.
   B. a treeless plain in an arctic region.
   C. a treeless plain in the West.
   D. a high cliff in the Rockies.

5. **"At first everything was going fine, but after three or four hours of traveling the worst happened." What was "the worst" that happened?**
   A. the tent was covered with snow
   B. Alexis broke her leg
   C. the dogs ran away
   D. Marty fell into a crevasse

6. **Why are Alexis and Marty on the tundra?**
   A. celebrating their wedding anniversary
   B. practicing for Marty's upcoming race
   C. practicing for Alexis' upcoming race
   D. advertising their outdoor equipment

7. **How far were Marty and Alexis from the town when Marty fell in the crevasse?**
   A. twelve miles  B. five miles  C. fourteen miles  D. twenty-four miles

8. **What equipment was used to rescue Marty?**
   A. snowmobiles and a sick sled
   B. ropes and ladders
   C. a train and fire truck
   D. ambulance and helicopter

9. **Which happened last?**
   A. it was dark and cold on the tundra...
   B. they found the tent nearly covered with snow...
   C. carrying her to town in record time...
   D. Marty gave Alexis a wink and smile...

*Total Correct*_____

# What Really Happened to Jack?

I'm Jack.
You know,
the same Jack
in that silly "Jack
and Jill" poem.
There's a little mis-
understanding about
what really happened
on that hill, which I want
cleared up. You see, I didn't
just fall down that hill by
accident.

It's like this. I was strolling down the road to the Moohaws' farm to borrow some eggs for my dad. He was making us omelets for breakfast and we were just two eggs shy. Anyway, I was walking along, minding my own busi- ness, when I looked up and saw Jill Moohaw coming toward me. My first thought was, "Run Jack, run!" My second, more sobering thought was, "There's no place to go, Jack," as there was a seven-foot fence on both sides of the road. Aughhhh!

"Hi Jack," Jill said to me in her most attractive voice.

"Uh...hi," I replied nervously.

You see, Jill is crazy about me. I'm not saying this to brag. It's the plain and scary truth. She had her heart set on little Jack Horner last year and drove him to stay in his corner. Now it appears it is my turn.

"Were you coming up to the farm?" she asked.

"Yes," I said.

"Oh, that's wonderful! You can help me **fetch** a pail of water. Come on!" she said, chasing me up the hill.

We went up the hill and filled the pail. I was itching to get out of there, so I turned to head back down when Jill started chasing after me. I dodged her attempt and started running down the trail as fast as my legs would allow. I turned to check my progress only to see her barreling down behind me, **shrieking** after me in her high pitched voice. It wasn't long before she caught up with me, and gave me a shove, which sent us both tumbling **chaotically** down the entire length of the hill.

I am now in bed, in **excruciating** pain, as I write this. I haven't seen Jill for a week. I think I kind of miss her.

# READING CHALLENGE

After reading "What Really Happened to Jack?," answer the following questions.

## Working with Vocabulary

Write the meaning for each word below.
1. shrieking _____
2. excruciating _____
3. chaotically _____
4. fetch _____

## Finding Details

5. Why was Jack going to the Moohaw's farm?

6. What was Jack's first thought when he saw Jill?

7. Who was Jill in love with last year?

8. How long has it been since Jack has seen Jill?

9. Why is Jack telling the story?

## Sequencing the Events

Number the sentences in the order in which they occurred in the story.

_____ You see, Jill is crazy about me.

_____ There's a little misunderstanding about what really happened on that hill. . .

_____ My first thought was, "Run Jack, run!"

_____ ". . .You can help me fetch a pail of water."

_____ We went up the hill and filled the pail.

_____ . . .we were just two eggs shy

## Checking Grammar

"We went up the hill and filled the pail."
10. What is the verb in the sentence?

11. The word hill is a noun. How is it used in the sentence?

12. What is the subject?

13. What part of speech is <u>up</u>?

14. What part of speech is <u>we</u>?

Remember, if you don't know what a word means, look it up in a dictionary! You'll do better in the exercises!

**Total Correct** _____

# The Canoe Trip

Early morning on the river,
fog and mist along the banks.
Sun behind the mountains,
and Dad sitting opposite me.

Planning for months
and the big day arrives.
Plenty of sunshine
and a summer of fun.

River is restless,
and I am too.
Anxious, a twelve-year-old boy,
canoeing the rapids.

My hero near me
to guide and help.
Experienced and strong,
he teaches me the same.

Deep in places and swift in others,
River sometimes is a bully.
Cautious and alert,
I know I can do this.

Nature sings
as I glide along the water.
Once a duck yelled
like a wounded dog.

Day not forgotten
and never will.
Memories carry me
like a canoe on the river.

# READING CHALLENGE

### After reading "The Canoe Trip," answer the following questions.

1. **The main idea of "The Canoe Trip" is most probably**
   A. planning is crucial for a twelve-year-old boy on the river.
   B. those good memories that guide and strengthen us in our lives.
   C. about a young boy who hears nature's calls to him on the river.
   D. the river is covered in mist and fog in the summertime.

2. **A word that means the opposite of the word anxious is**
   A. eager.          B. impatient.          C. loath.          D. excited.

3. **The "hero" of the young boy is**
   A. River.          B. Dad.          C. Nature.          D. Canoe.

4. **The following conclusion may be drawn after reading the poem.**
   A. The boy heard a duck yell as the boy canoed down the river.
   B. The boy's hero, the dad, was an average person in the boy's life.
   C. The boy had a great trip, which will always be in his memories.
   D. There was plenty of sunshine on the day of the canoe trip.

5. **"Once a duck yelled/like a wounded dog."  The word like suggests a**
   A. simile.          B. pun.          C. paradox.          D. metaphor.

6. **"Once a duck yelled/like a wounded dog."  Since a "duck" doesn't "yell," the writing technique is called a**
   A. personification.          B. simile.          C. pun.          D. metaphor.

7. **"Deep in places and swift in others,/River sometimes is a bully."  Because "River" is called a "bully," the writing technique is called**
   A. paradox.          B. metaphor.          C. irony.          D. simile.

8. **All but one of the following statements is true.**
   A. The boy is just as restless as the river.
   B. The river is treated as a person in the fifth stanza.
   C. The boy and his father are canoeing on a summer's morning.
   D.  It is raining as the boy and his father canoe the river.

**Total Correct** _____

# The Turn of Her Life

The stage is set.
Frozen and **shimmering** with each twinkle of light,
she appears from the shadows,
bringing the audience to their feet with delight.
The music begins.
With great beauty and style
she glides across the ice.
Graceful as a swan,
she moves eloquently about.
As the volume and pace increase,
she prepares for the turn of her life.
Dreams, once so far away,
now lay just beyond.
Taking flight, she soars as an eagle,
ending like a feather,
floating gently back to the frozen pond.

# READING CHALLENGE

**After reading "The Turn of Her Life," answer the following questions.**

1. **What is she doing in the poem?**
   A. roller skating     B. ice hockey     C. roller blading     D. ice skating

2. **In line 1, what is the stage?**
   A. frozen pond     B. sports arena     C. basketball court     D. ice arena

3. **In line 2, shimmering means**
   A. shivering.     B. giggling.     C. glowing.     D. waving.

4. **How does she "take flight?"**
   A. twisting and shouting     C. in an airplane
   B. turns and jumps     D. jumping off a cliff

5. **"Graceful as a swan. . ." is a**
   A. metaphor.     B. pun.     C. paradox.     D. simile.

6. **When she ends "like a feather," she**
   A. completes the turn and floats gently to the ice.
   B. hits the ice after leaping off the mountain.
   C. floats down from the building.
   D. falls slowly to her knees.

# Journal On Our Trip To New York City

July 15, 1999

My English teacher suggested I keep a journal this summer to record my ideas, experiences and reflections. This is my first journal, but the exercise seems to come naturally. I learn a lot about myself and the world around me through writing. Besides, if I turn my journal in to my teacher in the fall when school starts, I'll receive extra credit!

New York is a huge city. The number of people and buildings that occupy its crowded streets seem endless. Yesterday, my family and I took a tour around the city, which included a ferry ride to the Statue of Liberty. I didn't realize the statue is so tall. I wonder how the first immigrants to this country felt when they crossed the Atlantic Ocean to New York and saw the statue, standing tall and proud in the harbor they would call home. I don't understand why everyone in the world can't live in freedom. I'm glad I live in a country where I can live like I want to.

July 17, 1999

Today we are visiting the Metropolitan Museum of Art. I enjoy art, even though my own artistic skills aren't that great. Maybe I'll take a painting class at school next year. Aside from the museum, my favorite experience has been seeing the Broadway show, "The Lion King." It was great! I've seen the movie a million times, but it does not compare to the show. We were lucky to get tickets! I feel sorry for Simba. Losing his dad was so horrible. I would hate to lose my dad, because I think he's the most wonderful father in the world. I guess Simba felt the same way about his dad. Why can't people like Scar learn to live with everyone else? What is it about power that drives so many people to do awful things to each other?

July 20, 1999

I want to be an artist! I really do! Last Wednesday I went to another art museum. My art teacher, Mr. Trotter, would have been in heaven there.

I saw paintings by artists like Van Gogh, Matisse, Da Vinci, Monet, and many, many more whose names I can't remember. My favorite painting was by Matisse. I stared at the painting for a long time. In fact, my brother Jake kept poking me in the ribs and teasing me about it. "You're going to burn a hole in the picture if you'd don't stop staring," he said.

He can be really silly. Little brothers are like that. He's probably too young to appreciate fine art like Matisse's "Dance." It's an abstract painting of five women holding hands and dancing in a circle. I could almost sense their emotions, even though the painting is far from realistic, and primarily contains only three colors: blue, green and tan.

# READING CHALLENGE

**After reading "Journal On Our Trip To New York City," answer the following questions.**

1. **What does seeing the Statue of Liberty suggest to the writer of the journal?**
   A. vacationing with parents isn't as bad as some teenagers think
   B. living in a free and democratic society is great
   C. it would be nice to visit France
   D. people in New York are nuts

2. **Which journal entry is about Matisse's famous painting?**
   A. July 17, 1999
   B. July 16, 1999
   C. July 15, 1999
   D. July 20, 1999

3. **What is a main idea concerning Scar that the writer is expressing after seeing "The Lion King?"**
   A. money is evil
   B. power is always bad
   C. power shouldn't drive people to do bad things
   D. people like Scar should be imprisoned

4. **Who is the writer's art teacher?**
   A. Mr. Trotter
   B. Matisse
   C. Jake
   D. Van Gogh

5. **Who are some of the artists that the writer recognizes at the art museum?**
   A. Van Gogh, Matisse, Da Vinci, and Rembrandt
   B. Da Vinci, Van Gogh, Monet, Matisse
   C. Matisse, Monet, Van Gogh, Cezanne
   D. Monet, Da Vinci, Manet, Van Gogh

6. **Who is Jake?**
   A. a famous painting
   B. Mr. Trotter's favorite student
   C. no Jake is mentioned in the journal
   D. the writer's brother

Remember, if you don't know what a word means, look it up in a dictionary! You'll do better in the exercises!

*Total Correct*_____

# The Pond

When I open the lid to my bait box, I see a wide variety of rattletraps, spoonbaits, buzz-baits and other lures in a variety of different shapes, colors and sizes. Fishing is something I do all the time. It helps me relax and take the time to think about things.

My dad was the first person to take me fishing when I was five years old. We often went to a fishing hole within walking distance from our house, which we named, "The Pond." My first few times out, Dad had to tie the hook at the end of my line for me. I can do it myself now. He doesn't go with me on my fishing trips as much as he used to. He's busy with work and other things, and probably figures I'm old enough to handle it myself. However, though I like the independence and freedom, I miss his company sometimes. I still take the time to **reminisce** about the old days and the time we used to spend together.

Dad used to tell me that The Pond was extremely special. He said that a person who fishes can **contemplate** the universe in an afternoon. I had no idea what he was talking about at the time, but now that I'm older, I understand. One can contemplate the universe here because there's really nothing to do but cast a line, take in the scenery and think. Time seems to stand still at The Pond.

I rarely catch anything at The Pond, but I always come back, probably because it has made me a better and wiser person. I don't consider myself one of the smartest kids at school, but if you give me enough time, I can figure most everything out. Time is all a person needs to accomplish anything. I'm not rich, but I don't need money. I'm not especially popular, but I don't crave popularity either. All I need is The Pond. It gives me peace, relaxation and a sense of well-being.

Except for the grassy spot where I usually sit, The Pond is surrounded by mud. To the untrained eye, it's not a beautiful place. But if you give it a second chance, you'll notice all kinds of birds and animals, bugs, rocks and trees. This special place is most beautiful at night. As the moon shines off the top of the water, creating silver shadows on everything around, one can hear the **melodious** sounds of the crickets and frogs. Near The Pond's edge, a giant elm, older than me, stands alone, **chivalrously** casting its silver majesty over everything it touches.

I spend a great deal of time here, not because it is a great place to fish, but because this pond is the perfect place to sit, relax and think. If everyone had a place like this, I'm sure everybody would be much happier.

# READING CHALLENGE

### After reading "The Pond," answer the following questions.

## Working with Vocabulary

Write the meaning for each word below.

1. reminisce

2. contemplate

3. melodious

4. chivalrously

## Finding the Details

5. How old was the speaker when he first visited The Pond?

6. How far is the fishing hole from home?

7. What casts a "silver majesty" over The Pond?

8. Why does the speaker go to The Pond?

9. Has the speaker seen any animals near The Pond?

10. Who was the first person to take the speaker fishing?

11. What are two sounds heard at The Pond?

## Sequencing the Events

12. Number the sentences in the order in which they appear in the story.

_____ My first few times out, Dad had to tie the hook at the end of my line for me.

_____ ...one can hear the melodious sounds of the crickets and frogs.

_____ It gives me peace, relaxation and a sense of well-being.

_____ My dad was the first person to take me fishing when I was five years old.

_____ To the untrained eye, it's not a beautiful place.

_____ ...a person who fishes can contemplate the universe in an afternoon.

## Checking Grammar

"Near The Pond's edge, a giant elm, older than me, stands alone, chivalrously casting its silver majesty over everything it touches."

13. What is the subject in the above sentence?

14. "Near The Pond's edge," is called a
_____ phrase.

15. What is the verb?

16. What part of speech is <u>Pond's</u>?

# New School

Jack was a caring young man. He always gave of his time and labor in order to help a friend in need, and his friends thought kindly of him. He was the marvel of his eighth grade class at Selma Middle School; he was an honors student, gifted poet and talented artist. Lately, however, Jack was losing his focus. His creativity was waning, and he could not finish anything he started.

Jack's family had recently moved to Cataca Valley in Ohio from a medium-sized city in Arizona. His father had said the move would do Jack good, but Jack resented having to move in the middle of the school year.

Trying to make the best of situations, Jack presented himself as a happy person on the first day at his new school. He enjoyed his new teachers, and he met many new people that first day, but one girl in particular caught his eye.

Her name was Megan. She had a pretty face, and her eyes glowed with some inner pride that seemed to attract him to her. Feeling awkward and rather uncomfortable during the class discussions, Jack sat quietly and only spoke when he had to. He behaved this way in this class for a week before he finally developed the nerve to speak to Megan. She was shy also, and this certainly didn't help matters.

Megan's laugh was like music in his ears, her voice was like an angel's. During the first week, Jack and Megan probably spoke no more than twenty words to each other. It was difficult for Jack because he too was shy, and he didn't know what Megan found interesting. Furthermore, he had discovered that she lived only two blocks from him, but he was even too inhibited to walk past her house.

After Jack had been in school for about three weeks, Lyndsi Hamilton, one of Megan's friends, invited him to a party at her house the following weekend. At the party were about thirty kids from the seventh and eighth grade, including Mrs. Rowley, the eighth grade English teacher, and Megan. At first, Jack and Megan avoided each other, but the ice begin to break, and they left the party with each other's phone number.

Later that night at home, Jack composed a poem especially for Megan. He titled it, "You're Voice Is Where I Want to Be." Now he had to get the nerve to give it to her. Maybe at another party?

# READING CHALLENGE

### After reading "New School," answer the following questions.

1. The story is mainly about
   A. a party at Lyndsi's house.
   B. Megan and how she interacts with people around her.
   C. the seventh and eighth graders at Selma Middle School.
   D. adjustments and friendships.

2. Another word that means the same as incompetent is
   A. capable.
   B. useless.
   C. sad.
   D. worried.

3. Which of the following were at the party?
   A. Megan, Mrs. Rowley, Eliot
   B. Jack, Megan, Eliot
   C. Lyndsi, Jack, Megan
   D. Mrs. Rowley, Jon, Megan

4. Rowley was the last name for which of the following characters?
   A. English teacher
   B. Megan
   C. Jack
   D. Lyndsi

5. "Megan's voice was like an angel's." Because Megan's voice is compared to an angel's voice using the word like, this becomes a
   A. metaphor.
   B. paradox.
   C. simile.
   D. pun.

6. From where had Jack recently moved?
   A. Ohio
   B. Cataca
   C. Arizona
   D. New Jersey

7. According to the poem for which Jack wrote for Megan, where does he "want to be"?
   A. in her face
   B. near her voice
   C. ashes in her mind
   D. in heaven

8. All but one of the following is true about Jack.
   A. Jack was an honors student and a gifted poet.
   B. Jack seemed happy on his first day at his new school.
   C. Jack obtained Megan's phone number the third week of school.
   D. Jack was a talented artist, but he was shy with people.

9. A word that means the opposite of the word inhibited is
   A. withdrawn.
   B. outgoing.
   C. reserve.
   D. insecure.

Remember, if you don't know what a word means, look it up in a dictionary! You'll do better in the exercises!

# All I Can See

Although in my head
Are beaches and sand,
I open my eyes
To see only my hand.
It sits there quite nicely
On my paper so white,
But my teacher hath told me
A poem I must write.
My mind draws a blank,
No ideas are in sight.
I see only my hand
On my paper so white.
I write and erase,
Erase and I write.
Then into the garbage
My verse takes a flight.
Leaving only my hand,
And a fresh leaf of white.

# READING CHALLENGE

**After reading "All I Can See," answer the following questions.**

1. **The title of the poem suggests that**
   A. the writer can see clearly how to write the poem.
   B. the writer is blind and can't see.
   C. the writer can only see his/her hand on a blank sheet of paper.
   D. the writer can only see beaches and waves.

2. **In the last line, what is the leaf?**
   A. maple leaf                    C. white gold leaf
   B. sheet of white paper          D. sheet of gold paper

3. **The poem is mainly about**
   A. lacking ideas of what to write about.
   B. not being at the beach.
   C. having too many ideas to choose from.
   D. being bored at school.

4. **The expression, "verse takes a flight," means**
   A. the writer is taking a plane to read the poem at a convention.
   B. the poem disappears from the writer's mind.
   C. the writer awakens and forgets the poem.
   D. the poem is thrown into the trash.

**Total Correct**_____

# The Canopy

Slowly, Lilly folded the silky cloth into a neat square. It was the color of pink cotton candy, with ruffles on the edges. Every day since her third birthday, that cloth had been the last thing she saw before she fell asleep and the first thing she saw when she woke in the morning. For twelve years it had hung above her bed to make a canopy as she slept.

As Lilly stroked the cloth, memories of her childhood came

When she was nine, the canopy became a mosquito net that protected her from dangerous insects the size of cantaloupes on her African safari. When she was twelve, it was her canoe that floated her down the Amazon River. And at fourteen, it was her hot air balloon which sailed her over the Eiffel Tower in Paris.

Lilly had just recently turned sixteen. She was growing up and she wanted to act her age. For a long time she had felt that pink canopies were for little girls, but she had only recently convinced herself to take it down.

flooding back. Smiling, she recalled one night when she was five years old. It was one of those evenings she felt restless and was having trouble falling asleep. As a distraction, she pretended that her canopy bed was a covered wagon, under the stars at night. She pretended to be Laura Ingalls from "Little House on the Prairie."

On her eighth birthday, she had a slumber party, she remembered. Three of her best friends came over, and they spent the entire night under the canopy playing "truth or dare," whispering secrets to one another. What a night! But the next morning they were very tired.

With a sigh, she placed the canopy into her cedar chest and touched it one last time. Slowly she closed the lid and turned the key. Feeling a little overwhelmed, she lay down on her bed and looked up. Though she was sad that she was no longer a little girl, she looked forward to her future as a young woman. But as she closed her eyes, she heard the blasts of the jet engines getting ready to take her to the moon...

# READING CHALLENGE

### After reading "The Canopy," answer the following questions.

1. What is the main idea of "The Canopy?"

2. In three of four sentences, discuss something in your life that you may have outgrown.

3. Place the sentences below in sequence as they occur in the story.

_____With a sigh, she placed the canopy into her cedar chest.

_____But the next morning they were very tired.

_____Feeling a little overwhelmed, she lay down on her bed and looked up.

_____She was growing up and she wanted to act her age.

_____For twelve years it had hung above her head to make a canopy as she slept.

_____Smiling, she recalled one night when she was five years old.

## Finding Details

4. What adventure does Lilly recall experiencing when she was twelve?

5. How old is Lilly when she puts her canopy away for good?

6. When she was five, Lilly pretended to be what television character?

7. How old was Lilly when she flew over the Eiffel Tower in her "hot-air balloon?"

## Checking Grammar

"As Lilly stroked the cloth, memories of her childhood came flooding back."

8. What is the subject of the dependent clause?

9. What part of speech is <u>back</u>?

10. What is the subject of the independent clause?

**Total Correct**_____

# MY FAVORITE SPOT

Sometimes when I'm bored or lonely, I take the elevator to the top floor of our apartment building. Down the hall, there is a door that leads to a small stairway, which leads to another door opening to the roof. The roof is enclosed by a brick wall just short enough for me to see over. I have a favorite spot where I lean against the wall and look out across the city.

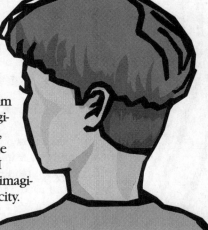

From high atop my building, I observe the noisy hustle and bustle of the streets and peak into the windows of nearby buildings, imagining the millions of people who **inhabit** them. Sometimes I catch a glimpse of someone watering their house plants, or talking on the phone. Quite often I'm entertained by the cat that regularly occupies the window ledge of an apartment lying almost at eye level across the street. Then there are times when the only thing that holds my attention is the endless sky.

But no matter what greets my hungry eyes from my perch on high, there's no limit to where my imagination can take me. I don't have mountains to climb, rivers to explore, or open fields to play in here in the city. But I do have a safe place to escape to, where I can contemplate the world around me. Sometimes imagination is all the room one needs, even in a crowded city.

# READING CHALLENGE

**After reading "My Favorite Spot," answer the following questions.**

1. **What is the main idea of the essay?**
   A. the city is better than the country
   B. spying on people is entertaining
   C. there is room for imagination, even in a crowded city
   D. the country is better than the city

2. **The term "hungry eyes" is an example of**
   A. a metaphor.                    C. a simile.
   B. personification.               D. a near rhyme.

3. **The writer visits his/her favorite spot when he/she**
   A. is bored or lonely.            C. is hungry.
   B. is angry.                      D. wants to be alone.

4. **The roof is enclosed by a wall made of**
   A. cement.        B. steel.        C. cinder block.        D. brick.

5. **A synonym for <u>inhabit</u> is**
   A. habitual.      B. inhibit.      C. dwell.        D. vacate.

# My English Journal

**September 15, 1999**

Mrs. Duncan wants us to write about the story we read last night and discussed today in class. The main character, Mr. Brawley, is a real crank. But he can't really help it because he's old and lonely. Jeremy, another character in the story, was wrong to make rude gestures and say hateful things about Mr. Brawley. It's much better to try to understand someone and their situation before passing judgment. There is an old man that lives two doors down from the house I grew up in. We would wave to him everyday as we passed by on our way to the bus stop, but he would never wave back. One day I was making fun of him, when my mom overheard us. She scolded me for being so callous, and explained that the old man was nearly blind, and probably couldn't see us wave. So, the next day we passed by his house, we voiced our "hello's," and to our surprise, he said hello back!

**September 17, 1999**

I learned to like reading this year. In English we read a story called "A Boy's Best Friend," by Isaac Asimov. It's a cool story about a boy, Jimmy, who lives on the moon with a mechanical dog named Robutt. One day Jimmy's father surprises him with a real dog he ordered from earth. The father thought Jimmy would be overjoyed with the gift, but Jimmy wasn't ready to give Robutt up. He loved his mechanical dog as much as anyone would love a real thing. Not seeming to understand, the father was ready to give the robot to someone else. He was certain the real dog would grow to love Jimmy. But what he didn't understand was the depth of feeling Jimmy had for Robutt. Even though Robutt was a machine with no emotions, Jimmy had strong feelings for him. And in the end, that was all that mattered.

**September 21, 1999**

Mrs. Duncan, my English teacher, suggested several books to read over the summer. The one that caught my attention is titled, "The Red Pony." It's about a ten-year-old boy who is given the present of his dreams — a red pony. He takes care of the pony and even begins to train it, but one day the pony dies of pneumonia after being left outside too long in the rain. Of course, Jody, the young boy, is **devastated**, having never faced such a loss in his short life. But his father promises to replace the pony with another if Jody works hard to save enough money for half the cost. I could really relate to this story, because it wasn't long ago that I lost my dog, Bo. I grew up with Bo, and he lived a long and happy life. When he died, I went behind the house to cry because I didn't want anyone to see me. I loved Bo so much.

# READING CHALLENGE

**After reading "My English Journal," answer the following questions.**

1. **The journal entry dated September 17, 1999 is mainly about**
   - A. not underestimating one's feelings for the objects they possess.
   - B. machines have feelings too.
   - C. robots can't replace pets.
   - D. humans are more important than machines.

2. **The word <u>devastated</u> means**
   - A. punished.
   - B  shattered.
   - C. handicapped.
   - D. elated.

3. **How does the writer feel about the elderly?**
   - A. Elderly people aren't polite.
   - B. Elderly people should be treated like children.
   - C. The elderly are just like everyone else and should be respected.
   - D. It's all right to be rude to elderly people if they're rude to you.

4. **What might one say Jody learned in "The Red Pony?"**
   - A. that ponies don't like the rain
   - B. promises are hard to keep
   - C. pets are replaceable
   - D. taking care of an animal is a big responsibility

5. **What happened to Bo?**
   - A. He ran away.
   - B. He died of old age.
   - C. He was hit by a car.
   - D. He died, and no further information is given.

6. **What does the journal suggest about the writer?**
   - A. The writer has a robot named Robutt.
   - B. The writer is a compassionate person.
   - C. The writer dislikes animals and elderly people.
   - D. The writer isn't a good student.

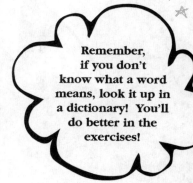

Remember, if you don't know what a word means, look it up in a dictionary! You'll do better in the exercises!

RBP

# A Visit

Feeling sorry for myself, I drove thirty miles in the pouring rain into the city to have my hair done. School wasn't going well, a co-worker was upset with me, and I had the flu. Nothing was going my way and I was in a horrible mood. But despite my downtrodden state of mind, I was looking forward to seeing Cindy. For several years she had cut my hair, and we had become good friends. No matter what mood I was in, Cindy always had a way of cheering me up.

When I entered the door to her salon, Cindy burst out laughing. After the sprint from the car to the building in the **torrential** downpour, I guess I looked pretty funny. She hugged me, led me to a chair and started shampooing my hair. I felt better even before the rinse.

However, my good mood was short-lived. Just as I decided that my problems were **tolerable**, Cindy started talking about an organization she had recently become involved with. It was an AIDS care team. She explained that the team was new and they worked with people who had the most severe cases of HIV infection. "While terminally ill people may find reason to be depressed, the man I was helping had a very upbeat outlook on life," she said.

She was deeply moved by the **optimism**, and positive outlook the man had. Everyday tasks held great meaning for him and he never used his sickness as an excuse not to live each day as best he could. When I asked her what her work involved, she said, "Just being a friend. I cut his hair and prepare dinner, or sometimes we just talk." Cindy explained that ever since he found out about his disease, the grass had suddenly became greener, music sounded clearer, and food even tasted better. One day, he told her that he wanted to watch the sunset over the water, so she took him to Belar's Landing where they had an **unobstructed** view of the horizon. "It was the most amazing sunset I've ever seen," said Cindy.

"How's he doing now?" I asked.

"He passed away a few weeks ago," she said, a faint smile crossing her face. "But he lived every day of his life."

Driving back home, all I could do was think of how self-absorbed I had been lately. I thought of Cindy and her incredible generosity, and I thought of her friend. I also thought of how great it was to be alive.

# READING CHALLENGE

### After reading "A Visit," answer the following questions.

1. The main idea of the story is

2. Place the sentences below in sequence as they occur in the story.

_____"the man I was helping had a very upbeat outlook on life..."

_____"He died a few weeks ago," she said...

_____school wasn't going well, a co-worker was upset with me...

_____"I cut his hair, and prepared him dinner, or sometimes we just talked."

_____However, my good mood was short-lived.

## Finding Details

3. What disease did the man whom Cindy was helping have?

4. Where did Cindy take the man to watch the sunset?

5. Why did the speaker drive to see Cindy?

6. What was the speaker's last thought?

## Working with Vocabulary

7. tolerable means

8. What is another word for unobstructed?

9. What is the opposite of optimism?

10. "Pertaining to a stream of water flowing with great force" is the definition for which word in the story?

## Reading to Think

11. Describe a time when you felt sorry for yourself. Did you have someone to cheer you up and help put things into perspective?

# The Secret

Unpacking a box of sweaters, Nancy Mason reflected on all the other times she spent packing and unpacking her belongings over the past ten years.

Nancy's father was an undercover detective and extremely devoted to his job. He was a remarkable detective, and was frequently used as a **decoy** to lure suspects. The downside to his job was the danger it involved. During a case, he and his family would move and even change their names to avoid revealing secret information. Nancy and her twin brother, Todd, liked their new home, and they hoped this case would last longer than most.

Within a few months, Nancy and Todd had become comfortable in their new surroundings and accustomed to their new names, Sonja and Jeff Ross. Nancy had made a few friends and had become particularly close to one girl, Becky Thomas, who was a cheerleader. While Todd, who made the football team, had become a valuable player. Both Sonja and Jeff liked living in Eastwood.

As best friends, Nancy and Becky naturally told each other everything. Nancy knew that the case her father was working on would soon come to an end. And she was wary of the fact that she would again be forced to leave her friends behind.

Aware of his family's growing attachment to their new life in Eastwood, Mr. Mason applied for a permanent job with the police station in town. He loved his current job, but he valued his family's happiness over anything. He decided to withhold the news from his family, as there was only a **minuscule** chance that a job would become available.

The Masons lived in Eastwood three years. Mr. Mason's case was coming to a close, and still he hadn't been offered a permanent job. Todd and Nancy would be entering Eastwood High in the fall if they stayed.

Three weeks before Mr. Mason's case was schedule to come to an end, he received a late-night phone call from Chief Inspector Jones. He spoke with the chief for a few minutes, and was **elated** when he hung up. Mr. Mason had never revealed to anyone in the family that he had been searching for a permanent position, so when Todd overheard his father agreeing to sign papers the following morning, he feared the worst. Seeing the look of dismay on Todd's face, Mr. Mason quickly informed him of the good news.

They then woke Nancy and told her. Needless to say, there was quite a celebration in the Mason house that evening! Finally, they had a permanent home and no further need for secret identities.

# READING CHALLENGE

### After reading "The Secret," answer the following questions.

1. **As the story unfolds, Nancy is**
   A. writing a letter to her friend Becky.
   B. unpacking a box of sweaters.
   C. sorting out old letters from friends.
   D. unpacking a box of books.

2. **A <u>decoy</u> means**
   A. lure.          B. prediction.          C. uniformed police.          D. promotion.

3. **How long did the Masons live in Eastwood before Mr. Mason found a permanent job?**
   A. ten years          B. two years          C. three years          D. twelve years

4. **The secret was**
   A. Nancy's father was a criminal.
   B. Nancy's mother had a drinking problem.
   C. Nancy's brother had been in a juvenile home.
   D. Nancy's father was an undercover cop.

5. **<u>Minuscule</u> means**
   A. small.          B. average.          C. better.          D. good.

6. **Nancy and Todd's new names in Eastwood were**
   A. Sonja and Jack Ross.          C. Sandra and Jeff Ross.
   B. Sonja and Jeff Ross.          D. Sonja and Joe Ross.

7. **How did Todd discover his dad's secret?**
   A. he read it on a piece of paper
   B. his mother told him
   C. he overheard his dad talking on the phone
   D. the chief told him

8. **<u>Elated</u> means**
   A. satisfied.          B. content.          C. upset.          D. exhilarated.

9. **In the fall, Nancy and Todd will be entering**
   A. Eastville High School.          C. Eastwood Elementary School.
   B. Eastwood Middle School.          D. Eastwood High School.

10. **Which came last?**
    A. a celebration
    B. Mr. Mason received a new job
    C. Todd made the football team
    D. Nancy became friends with Becky

# FOUR-WHEELER FISHING TRIP

My name is John Lankershire, and I'm thirteen years old. I have one brother, Rhett, who is eleven and we're both out of school for eight weeks enjoying the summer. Rhett and I are rarely bored and almost always up to something. Yesterday was no exception.

We enjoy fishing on Smith Lake, especially during the summer. Our dad has taken us there many times because he enjoys fishing as much as we do. The lake, about fifteen minutes from our house, is too far for Rhett and I to walk. So yesterday we decided to take dad's four-wheeler.

The trip took us about an hour because we stopped to watch two groundhogs on the side of the road. They were standing upright, holding something with their front paws, and chewing whatever it was from time to time. They looked mechanical and **detached** from everything around them, as if they were concerned about nothing but their next meal.

Arriving at the lake, we found our usual spot and fished for about five minutes before disaster struck. Because I was so excited and eager to get fishing, I had left the four-wheel-er in neutral. There was nothing to stop it from rolling because it wasn't in gear. Before we knew it, the four-wheeler was rolling rapidly down the bank heading straight for the water! There was nothing we could do. With a loud "splash," it hit the water and immediately began to sink. Rhett and I stood and stared hopelessly for awhile, unable to believe what had just happened.

Collecting myself, I asked "What are we going to do now?" The four-wheeler was now completely submerged and couldn't be **discerned** at all. Rhett didn't know what to do anymore than I did.

Suddenly, we both jumped into the lake and tried to pull the four-wheeler from the murky water by hand. But it was too heavy and had already sunk too far.

"Now what?" asked Rhett, **exasperated**.

"There's nothing we can do, but walk to the nearest cabin, call Dad and tell him what happened. I hope he's not too angry," I said, as we slowly turned to face our fates.

# READING CHALLENGE

### After reading "Four-Wheeler Fishing Trip," answer the following questions.

1. The story is mainly about

2. Place the sentences in sequence as they occur in the story.

_____"What are we going to do now?"

_____. . .it was too heavy and had already sunk too far.

_____We enjoy fishing on Smith Lake, especially during the summer.

_____"I hope he's not too angry."

_____. . .we stopped to watch two groundhogs on the side of the road.

## Finding Details

3. Who is telling the story?

4. Where did John and Rhett go fishing?

5. Why did the four-wheeler roll into the lake?

6. How did the boys travel to Smith Lake?

7. What did Rhett and John stop to look at on their trip to the lake?

## Working with Vocabulary

8. **Exasperated** means

9. What is another word for <u>detached</u>?

10. What is a synonym for the word <u>discerned</u>?

## Reading to Think

11. Write about a time when you did not think or act responsibly.

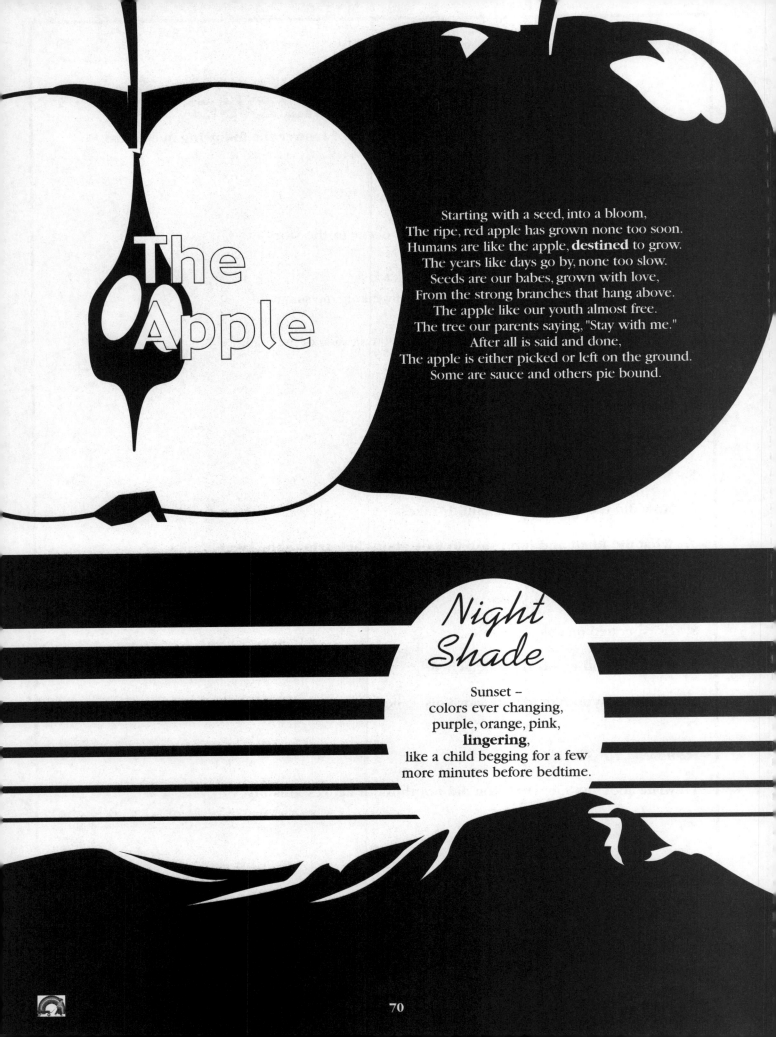

# The Apple

Starting with a seed, into a bloom,
The ripe, red apple has grown none too soon.
Humans are like the apple, **destined** to grow.
The years like days go by, none too slow.
Seeds are our babes, grown with love,
From the strong branches that hang above.
The apple like our youth almost free.
The tree our parents saying, "Stay with me."
After all is said and done,
The apple is either picked or left on the ground.
Some are sauce and others pie bound.

# Night Shade

Sunset –
colors ever changing,
purple, orange, pink,
**lingering**,
like a child begging for a few
more minutes before bedtime.

# READING CHALLENGE

### After reading "The Apple," and "Night Shade," answer the following questions.

1. "The Apple," is mainly about
   A. picking apples too soon.
   B. how humans are like an apple.
   C. how some people grow apples.
   D. the value of apples.

2. "Like a child begging for a few minutes..." is an example of a
   A. simile.
   B. pun.
   C. metaphor.
   D. hyperbole.

3. **Destined** means
   A. doomed.
   B. unable.
   C. predetermined.
   D. fertilized.

4. **In line 8 of "The Apple," who are the parents?**
   A. apple
   B. sunset
   C. babes
   D. tree

5. **Lingering** means
   A. to loiter.
   B. to smell.
   C. to talk.
   D. to snicker.

6. "Night Shade" is mainly about
   A. dirty windows.
   B. a beautiful sunset.
   C. going to bed.
   D. a beautiful sunrise.

7. In the poem "Night Shade," what three colors are used to describe the changing sun?

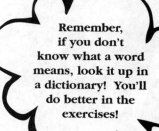

Remember, if you don't know what a word means, look it up in a dictionary! You'll do better in the exercises!

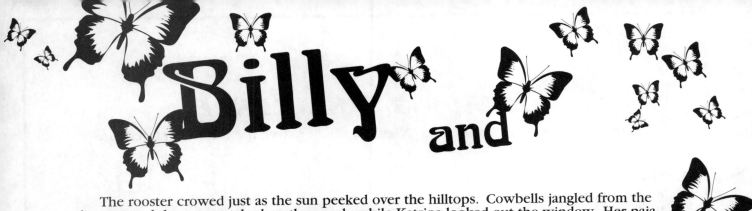

# Billy and

The rooster crowed just as the sun peeked over the hilltops. Cowbells jangled from the distance and the cat stretched on the porch, while Katrina looked out the window. Her pajamas clung to her, wet with sweat. She wiggled out from underneath the heavy blankets and placed her bare feet onto the dusty wood floor.

A black cotton dress hung on a nail in the wall. From her dresser drawers she pulled out thick, wool socks and a cotton undershirt. Katrina put on her clothes and looked into the cracked mirror. She tried in **vain** to brush her brown hair into a bun at the base of her head. Failing, she fastened a white bonnet to her head instead.

In the kitchen, Katrina's mother was toasting some wheat bread over the fire and frying eggs in a skillet. A single candle dimly lit the entire room. Within ten minutes the whole Albers family came together for their morning meal.

Samuel Albers, Katrina's father, announced over breakfast that the family would be going to the Smallwoods' house for supper that night. It would take at least four hours to travel there, so as soon as breakfast was over and the table cleared, everyone began making preparations for the journey. Katrina helped her mother fry some apples and bake cornbread. Her brother John tended to the horses and wagon. Her two younger sisters were busy in their room, packing and talking quietly. Everyone packed the items they would need for an overnight stay.

Even with all the hustle and bustle, Katrina was preoccupied with something else — the **monotony** of her life. Katrina felt that she had little to look forward to and at least once a week, Katrina had been crying herself to sleep at night, longing to be somewhere else. She was almost sixteen and she needed more freedom and less demands from her family. Furthermore, she had no friends, except for Billy and the butterflies.

Billy lived nearby. Katrina met him frequently behind the old barn to talk and to look for butterflies. It was their favorite pastime. She had known him for years, but it wasn't until eight months ago that they began to spend a lot more time together. She had developed somewhat of a crush on him over the last few months. He was always polite, he listened to her, he knew everything about butterflies and she had learned to trust him with all her heart.

Katrina had an obsession with butterflies. She longed to fly and to be free just like they were. When she was younger, she constantly chased them in the yard and fields, just as she chased freedom in her mind. Unlike her two sisters, Katrina had never totally yielded to the **constraints** of her family and their conservative ways.

Katrina was shaken from this reverie by her father's voice. "Let's go Katrina. Load 'em up!" he shouted. She slowly picked up her bags, closed the door behind her and made her way to the wagon where everyone was patiently waiting. The sturdy wagon

# the Butterfly

was spacious and even with a family their size, there was room so everyone could spread out and relax.

Katrina must have dozed off, because it seemed like only minutes had passed before they arrived at the Smallwoods' large, two-story house. Her eyes slowly adjusted to the light, and she noticed that on the porch sat some foreigners, who had probably come to buy baskets and preserves from the Smallwoods.

Entering the house and climbing the stairs to the bedroom she would be sharing with her friend, Alice Smallwood, Katrina stopped. She thought she had seen a yellow and black butterfly dancing on the landing halfway up the stairs. She rushed to the room and dumped her bags, immediately returning to the landing. By this time, the butterfly was **descending** the stairs, and Katrina did the same. She was about fourteen stairs from the first floor when she got close enough to the butterfly to touch it. But when she reached for it, she lost her footing and tumbled down the steep stairs to the bottom.

Although she was knocked unconscious for a few minutes, she didn't get hurt. Still, her family was terribly worried. The Smallwoods felt responsible because the accident had happened in their home. They were very **apologetic**, and Katrina was grateful. But what she really wanted was to be left alone. Several of the many guests who had been invited for dinner started to arrive, and Katrina didn't want to cause a scene or make a fuss.

To put her at ease, the Smallwoods set her up in a makeshift day bed in one of the back rooms. Some of the girls her age, who had been invited with their families, came into the room for a visit. But no one seemed to be able to make her smile. Sensing something was wrong, Katrina's mother and father scanned the party for Billy's parents, whom they knew had also been invited to the party. They decided that their rules against socializing with young men could be overlooked this evening if it meant Katrina would feel better. It wasn't long before they tracked down Billy, and took him into the room to visit, and hopefully cheer up, Katrina. When they entered the room, Katrina was facing a window and didn't hear them approach.

"Katrina, we have a surprise visitor for you," said her father. She turned from the window to see Billy standing in the doorway. Immediately, a huge smile appeared on her face. Billy began walking towards her. Katrina was surprised at her parents' kind gesture and did not know how to respond. Without a word, Billy sat next to her. And then, opening his hands, the beautiful black and yellow butterfly which Katrina had chased earlier magically appeared. The butterfly spread its wings and fluttered around and around Katrina's head. All she could do was smile.

73

RBP

# READING CHALLENGE

**After reading "Billy and the Butterfly," answer the following questions.**

1. **The story is mainly about**
   A. a strict family.
   B. restlessness and growing up.
   C. Billy and insects.
   D. a love affair.

2. **<u>Apologetic</u> means**
   A. regretful.
   B. hypnotized.
   C. responsible.
   D. elated.

3. **The story suggests that Katrina feels her life is <u>monotonous</u> because**
   A. Billy won't marry her.
   B. her parents don't love her.
   C. she needs more freedom.
   D. butterflies are all the same color.

4. **Katrina had an obsession with**
   A. butterflies.
   B. her friend, Alice Smallwood.
   C. breakfast.
   D. reading and studying about insects.

5. **The opposite of <u>descending</u> is**
   A. rising.
   B. riding.
   C. plunging.
   D. falling.

6. **The Albers family was going to the Smallwoods' house for**
   A. a wedding.
   B. supper.
   C. a funeral.
   D. a picnic.

7. **What caused Katrina to become unconscious?**
   A. she fell from a high ridge
   B. she almost drowned in a lake
   C. she tumbled down the stairs
   D. she fell out of the wagon

8. **What happened last?**
   A. Katrina met him frequently behind the old barn to talk and to look for butterflies.
   B. She rushed to the room and dumped her bags...
   C. cowbells jangled from the distance
   D. She turned from the window to see Billy...

9. **"Unlike her two sisters, Katrina had never totally yielded to the <u>constraints</u> of her family and their conservative ways."**

   **How is <u>constraints</u> used in this sentence?**
   A. controls
   B. bondage
   C. requests
   D. freedom

10. **"She tried in <u>vain</u> to brush her brown hair into a bun."**

    **How is <u>vain</u> used in this sentence?**
    A. with too much pride
    B. piece of metal to show which way the wind is blowing
    C. without much luck
    D. with success

Remember, if you don't know what a word means, look it up in a dictionary! You'll do better in the exercises!

*Total Correct* _____

# The Sky

Bright, dazzling sunlight fills the sky,
**glimmering** upon the water.
Colors of gold, red, and
majestic purple clothe the clouds
with a garment of **shimmering** silk.

The sky darkens
and a gentle hush falls over the land.
The world full of **awe**, silently watches,
as the sun goes softly to sleep
in the open, loving arms
of the **sea**.

# READING CHALLENGE

### After reading "Perfect Love," answer the following questions.

1. In line 9, what figure of speech is used when the sun goes "softly to sleep?"
   A. simile          B. personification     C. metaphor          D. pun

2. What is the root word of <u>shimmering</u>?

## Working with Vocabulary

3. Which word in the poem matches the definition:  <u>any article of clothing</u>?
   A. softly          B. silk          C. garment          D. hush

4. <u>Awe</u> means:

5. A word in the poem that means "glimmering," or "glowing," is

6. A synonym for <u>majestic</u> is

7. What is another spelling of the word "sea," and what does it mean?

## Writing to Think

8. Create an image or short poem in which you use personification (a writing technique in which an inanimate object is given human-like characteristics).

**Total Correct**_____

# An Exercise in Futility

I'm standing on the soccer field,
looking left to right,
for one of the forwards to yield
a perfect pass that night.

I saw him in the open,
the new guy who just got here.
He is ready to jump in
on the goalie who is near.

I make the perfect pass to him.
He receives the ball and shoots.
No one knows if it will go in.
He didn't wear his lucky boots.

As the ball sinks into the net,
we should have known he would score.
With a pass like that, it's a sure bet,
like walking through an open door.

The crowd was jumping wildly
in the excitement of the shot.
Someone might say mildly,
but I should think not!

He wanted to thank me
after the game
for being the key
that brought him his fame.

He walked up with a grin
and said, "thanks for the pass."
Placing my thumb on my chin,
I said, "I'll see you in class."

Suddenly, I heard a shout.
Someone said, "Wake up, Andy!"
A daydream — what was this all about?
Still at school — this is just dandy.

# READING CHALLENGE

**After reading "An Exercise in Futility," answer the following questions.**

1. **Futility** means
   A. usefulness.
   B. useless.
   C. importance.
   D. sportsmanship.

2. **Who is the word "he" referring to in the poem?**
   A. the new kid
   B. Andy
   C. the coach
   D. someone in the crowd

3. **When "he," walked up to "I," what did "he" say?**
   A. I'll see you in class
   B. Wake up, Andy
   C. throw me the ball
   D. thanks for the pass

4. **When the poem concludes, we discover that it's actually a**
   A. true story.
   B. nightmare.
   C. daydream.
   D. dramatic play.

5. **In which line of the poem are we told the name of the sport?**
   A. line 13
   B. line 1
   C. line 9
   D. line 26

6. **In the poem what did the speaker do that enabled the team to win?**
   A. he put his thumb on his chin
   B. he receives the ball and shoots
   C. he walks up with a grin
   D. he makes the perfect pass

**Total Correct** _____

# DoZZzING

Can't they ever be quiet?
Won't they ever shut up?
My eyelids are getting tight
Like a sleepy little pup.

My head falls over.
My! What a bore!
I'm out like a light.
I begin to snore.

Suddenly, there's a jab at my side.
My eyelids pop open ever so wide.
I hate to be rude,
I think I just need food.

The speaker is finished
And I am called on next.
I jump out of my seat
As a natural **reflex**.

I can't be that boring, I thought to myself,
With more information straight off the shelf.
Confidence and determination,
I take my mighty station.

As I am reading
My bubble is popped.
For when I glance up,
All heads are dropped!

# READING CHALLENGE

### After reading "Dozing," answer the following questions.

1. "Like a sleepy little pup" in line 4 is an example of a
   A. metaphor.
   B. simile.
   C. pun.
   D. hyperbole.

2. What is the meaning of <u>reflex</u> in line 16?
   A. decline
   B. glimpse
   C. gimmick
   D. response

3. Why is the speaker's bubble popped?


4. The speaker comments, "I can't be that boring,. . ." What reason does the speaker give for not boring the listeners?
   A. The speaker has information straight off the shelf.
   B. The speaker has self confidence and candy for everyone.
   C. The speaker has determination and plenty of handouts.
   D. The speaker has information straight from the computer.

5. In the second stanza, what is the simile?
   A. begin to snore
   B. what a bore
   C. like a light
   D. head falls over

## Checking Grammar

"Suddenly, there's a jab at my side."

6. What is the subject of this sentence?


7. What is the verb in the sentence?


8. What part of speech is suddenly?

Remember, if you don't know what a word means, look it up in a dictionary! You'll do better in the exercises!

**Total Correct**_____

# Friends

If I could have traded places with anyone in the world, it would have been with Hannah NeSmith. She was pretty, popular, and intelligent, and everyone liked her. I considered myself lucky to have her as my best friend.

Most people would probably never imagine the two of us even speaking to each other. In my opinion, I am just your average girl. My name is plain, my grades are mediocre, and my looks are definitely not sought after by any world class photographer. Although when I was a baby my mother entered my picture into a baby contest and I did receive honorable mention!

Even though I liked Hannah a great deal, there was no **envy** in our friendship. We considered ourselves equals, each having our faults, and each having our strengths. I have to admit, Hannah could not throw a football quite like me, but on the other hand I doubt if she ever cared.

Sometimes I asked Hannah why she liked me as her best friend, and she always answered by asking me why I liked her. We were just meant to be friends.

Hannah and I spent all of our time together. Sometimes I think it would have been easier if she had just moved into our house. It would have been more convenient than sending her home just to take a shower every day! Our parents didn't seem to agree with this, however. They thought that at least every other weekend should be devoted to "family time" when each of our families could spend time separately.

On the weekends not taken up by "family time," Hannah and I would go to the mall. Two months ago we had a facial just for fun. She looked like one of those runway models who make millions of dollars off their looks. The makeup complemented her dark hair and eyes perfectly. She looked beautiful! I, on the other hand,

looked like a clown ready for a guest appearance on a late night television show. At least I would make people laugh!

Hannah's sixteenth birthday party was a blast. My sixteenth doesn't come for another six months. Her backyard was packed full of family and friends. Her parents surprised her by giving her a car. Immediately, she began talking about all the places we would go and all the things we could do now that she had a car. I was just as excited as she was because we always had fun together. However, I knew my parents. They would not be excited about the idea of just Hannah and I driving to the mall and everywhere else we intended to go.

It didn't take long for Hannah to get her driver's license. She scored perfectly on the driving test. Eventually, my parents **rescinded** their decision and decided that it was safe for me to ride with Hannah. However, it was embarrassing when my parents asked Hannah if they could ride with her to check out her driving skills.

Our first long distance trip was to the mall about twenty-five miles from our small town of Manchester. That night, as I waited for Hannah to pick me up, I began to feel incredibly independent for the first time in my life. My parents were finally trusting me! Of course, when Hannah arrived, they still did what I expected, lecturing us on car safety, traffic signals and passing other automobiles. I believe now that they were trying to scare us from going because they went on and on and on. Finally, we were out the door.

Hannah was a good driver. She obeyed all the traffic laws, never attempting to speed or show off. On the way, we discussed our dreams and goals and how quickly we were growing up. She seemed to be so **sentimental** as we drove along. Now that we had our independence, we were both feeling the **reality** of the additional responsibilities which came with being on our own.

After shopping at the mall, we ate dinner and headed home. It was later than we thought so we called our parents on my mobile phone to let them know we were on our way.

We arrived home safe and sound. Our great adventure was over. Hannah, of course, spent the night at my house. We had to plan where we were going the next day.

How does the ocean sound? How about New York? San Francisco? Monterey Bay...

# READING CHALLENGE

### After reading "Friends," answer the following questions.

1. The story is mainly about

2. Number the sentences in order in which they occurred in the story.

    _____She scored perfectly on the driving test.

    _____We had to plan where we were going the next day.

    _____My name is plain, my grades are mediocre, and my looks are definitely . . .

    _____Hannah's sixteenth birthday party was a blast.

    _____She looked like one of those runway models who make millions . . .

3. In the story, another word for <u>took back</u> is

4. ". . . there was no envy in our friendship."  In this sentence <u>envy</u> means

5. The quality or condition of being <u>actual</u> or <u>true</u> is the definition for _____.

6. What was the first place Hannah and the author drove to?

7. Having or showing delicate and tender feelings is the definition for _____.

8. What did Hannah do at the end of the story?

9. In what town do Hannah and the author live?

10. Why do you think the speaker keeps mentioning the fact that she thinks Hannah is so beautiful?

### Reading to Think

11. On a separate sheet of paper, list ten characteristics that you look for in a friend.
    Example: *Always willing to listen.*

# There's A Cannibal

"I'm bored out of my mind!" said Roger to his mom one summer afternoon.

"Saying you're bored means you have no internal resources," she replied. "It's a beautiful summer day. There are plenty of things to do. Use your imagination."

"But I want to go camping, and Dad can't go with us this weekend. Why won't you let George and I go alone?" pleaded Roger. But no amount of **imploring** would change her mind. Roger's mom explained to him that at eleven, he was still too young to camp unaccompanied by an adult. Visibly upset, Roger turned to leave the room. Just then, an idea occurred to him.

"What if George and I camp in the backyard?" he asked his mother. She readily agreed and in just a few hours Roger and his friend George had set up a tent with their sleeping bags. They were making last minute adjustments to the tent when it started to get dark outside. When night did finally arrive, the boys cooked food on their camp stove, roasted marshmallows and told stories in the moonlight. But still, Roger wasn't satisfied with his camping adventure. It just wasn't like camping in the wilderness. Where was the excitement? A great camp-out involved **exploration** and adventure.

"I have another idea," said Roger, who had decided that for this camp-out to be successful, they needed to use their imaginations a little bit more. They decided to venture around the backyard without their flashlights and pretend they were in a jungle with tall grass and animals. The garden hose suddenly became a mighty python which hissed and snapped at their feet as they tried to cross the backyard. Finally, after dodging the poisonous fangs, which seemed to be about two feet long, they found themselves dashing to the far corner of their wild kingdom to escape a prowling tiger which moments before was meowing for its owner. But in the end, it was the tribe of cannibals that almost had them running for the warmth and safety of their own beds. Earlier, they had been harmless shrubbery carved into odd shapes and sizes by Roger's father the weekend before. Now, Roger and George found themselves pleading to them for mercy and begging for their very lives! Finally, after George threw

# In My Backyard!

himself at the feet of the chief cannibal and begged him to let them go so they could go fight an evil king in Africa, the two boys were released and sent on their way. However, they did not leave before the chief presented them with special hunting spears to take with them on their long journey.

It was approaching midnight, and the two boys were almost back to their tent when they confronted their greatest challenge of all. A huge, beautiful lioness was looking for her lost cub. Her mighty roar could be heard all over the jungle, echoing from the hills down to the waterfalls.

Suddenly, both boys realized that Roger's mom was standing on the back porch yelling at them to get inside the tent and go to sleep. "You're going to wake up the entire neighborhood!" she said before turning on her heel and stomping back inside.

Settling into the tent and drifting off to sleep, Roger began to dream of far off places and events. There seemed to be no end to their adventures. Tomorrow they would set sail for Africa!

# READING CHALLENGE

**After reading "There's A Cannibal In My Backyard!," answer the following questions.**

1. What is the main idea of this story?

2. Number the sentences to show the order in which they happened in the story.

_____It was approaching midnight, and the two boys were almost back...

_____They were making last minute adjustments to the tent when...

_____But no amount of imploring would change her mind.

_____"You're going to wake up the entire neighborhood!"

_____"I'm bored out of my mind!" said Roger...

_____...the boys cooked food on their camp stove, roasted marshmallows and...

_____Tomorrow they would set sail for Africa!

## Finding Details

3. In this story, the garden hose became a_____.

4. Where did Roger plan on going on his next adventure?

5. Roger and George's greatest challenge was a huge, beautiful _____.

6. A great camp-out involves what two things?

7. The tribe of _____ almost had them running for the warmth and safety of their own beds.

## Working with Vocabulary

8. "A great camp-out involved <u>exploration</u> and adventure."  Choose a word that means the same as the underlined word.
   A. discovery          B. explanation          C. campfire          D. food

9. What is a synonym for the word <u>imploring</u>.
   A. imploding          B. pleading          C. discouraging          D. reproaching

## Checking Grammar

10. "Settling into the tent and drifting off to sleep, Roger began to dream of far off places and events."  What is the subject of this sentence?
    A. settling          B. places          C. Roger          D. tent

11. What is the verb in the above sentence (question #10)?
    A. settling          B. drifting          C. sleep          D. began

*Total Correct*_____

# FATE OVER CHOCOLATE PIE

Last night, fate determined someone would die
over my mother's delicious chocolate cream pie.
A desperate robber was in the house,
when he was surprised by a quiet, small mouse.

While he was screaming, everyone was dreaming.
And when we woke, we found a plate filled with pie o'erstreaming.
There was the robber, lying on the floor where he stopped short of the door.
Likely, he died of panic. Seems he was a chocolate fanatic.

RBP

# WRITING CHALLENGE

After reading "Fate Over Chocolate Pie," use your own imagination to write a poem or short story about your favorite dessert. From *banana splits* to *Key Lime Pie*, any dessert will do. After writing your poem or story, decorate the page to make it even more irresistible. Have fun!

# Focus

Laura buried her head further into her pillow. The only sounds to break the silence of her empty bedroom were her sobs, which bounced off the walls like ping pong balls.

"What is wrong with me?" Laura asked herself. "Why is everything so complicated? Why am I so unhappy?"

Laura took her pillow and pulled it over her head. The room began to spin as images of her life flashed before her eyes...

In Mrs. Johnson's scribbled hand writing a big red C- on Laura's history test fluttered before her eyes. Laura had studied so hard for that test, harder then she had ever studied before. Still, her grade was far from satisfactory and she did not know why. She had never received so many C's from a teacher in her life and now Laura felt that the only reason why had to be because Mrs. Johnson did not like her. There was no other reason.

Laura rolled over and stared at the ceiling. Tears continued to roll of her tender cheeks. "And now," she thought to herself, "I am losing my best friend too."

A smile escaped from the corner of her mouth as she pictured her friend, Amanda. It vanished just as quickly when she remembered that after tomorrow, she might never see her again.

Laura and Amanda had been best friends all of their lives. They had met the summer between first and second grade while Laura and her parents were on vacation in New York. At that time, Amanda lived in New York City with her mother, Gail. The two girls had met on a playground in Central Park while their mothers sat on a park bench and talked all afternoon. The next year Laura's mother hired Gail to manage an advertising agency near their home in Los Angeles. This was the greatest news both Laura and Amanda had ever heard! With their mother's working together they would now get to see each other all the time, and they did! They went to school together, they worked at the same sandwich shop during the summer, they even took ballet lessons together at the same dance studio! Nothing could separate the two, until now. Amanda's mother was taking another job in Seattle, Washington and the new position starts immediately.

"Why me?" Laura asked herself. "Why is my life falling apart?" Just then there was a knock on the door. "Come in," Laura sobbed as the door swung open. "Mom!" She cried as her mother walked into the bedroom and leaned down to give her a hug. The warmth and strength of her mother's arms made Laura sob even harder. She never wanted her mother to let go.

An hour later Laura finished telling her mother why her life was falling apart. With no more strength, Laura laid her head back onto the pillow as a single tear escaped her red, swollen eyes. She was exhausted, and even though it felt great to have her mother at her side, Laura still felt very empty. Nothing made sense.

"Laura, look at me," her mother said. "I know things are tough right now, but I need you to remember that everything makes sense in our lives sooner or later. The important thing is not to lose focus on who you are and what you want to accomplish. See that over there?" She pointed to a glass ballerina that hung from the ceiling of Laura's room. "Remember when you were in ballet and you were practicing your **pirouettes**?"

Laura nodded her head slowly. "We were supposed to pick one thing and focus on it so we wouldn't lose track of where we were when we spun around."

"Exactly!" Laura's mother exclaimed. "It's called finding your focus. Honey, you are a wonderful and talented person, but if you lose sense of who you are and what you are doing, then it is very easy to lose control and become dizzy and confused. Picking a spot and focusing isn't just for ballet, but for everything in life. I love you and so do a lot of other people. Remember that you are never alone. Concentrate and really focus on what is important to you. Everything else will take care of itself."

Laura's mother then stood up and headed for the door.

"Mom."

"Yes, honey."

"Thanks. Not only for saying all that stuff to me, but also for being my mother. I'll never forget my 'focus' again!" After her mom left the room, Laura looked back up at the ballerina twirling from her ceiling. It had been there for years, but she had become so oblivious to it that she had forgotten that it was even up there. Another smile now spread across her face. This one, however, was different. Laura now smiled because she realized that no matter how lost she may feel, she would never have to look far to find herself, nor her interests, again.

# READING CHALLENGE

### After reading "Focus," answer the following questions.

1. **How old is Laura?**
   A. 21          B. 12          C. does not say          D. 14

2. **What was the first image that "flashed before" Laura's eyes?**
   A   Meeting Amanda in New York
   B   Her mother coming into her room
   C   Mrs. Johnson's scribbled hand writing
   D   A glass ballerina hanging from her ceiling

3. **Which of the following is a simile:**
   A   her sobs which bounced off the walls like ping pong balls.
   B   The warmth and strength of her mother's arms...
   C   "It's called finding your spot."
   D   Laura still felt very empty.

## Sequence of Events

4. **Place the sentences in sequence as they occur in the story.**

   Another smile now spread across her face.

   Laura's mother than stood up and headed for the door.

   Laura took her pillow and pulled it over her head.

   Laura rolled over and stared at the ceiling.

## Finding Details

5. **Where did Laura and Amanda work together during the summer?** _____
6. **What was hanging from Laura's ceiling?** _____
7. **What did Laura practice in ballet?** _____
8. **Laura never wanted to let what person go?** _____

## Working with Vocabulary

8. **What is the definition of** <u>pirouette</u>? **Use it in a complete sentence below.**

# GRAMMAR GUIDE

Use this quick reference chart to answer your grammatical questions

## A comma is used . . .
✔ to separate words, phrases, or clauses in a series (at least three items)

✔ to set off a direct quotation

✔ after greetings or salutations in a letter

✔ after the words "yes" and "no" when they begin a sentence

✔ to separate the names of a city and state in addresses

✔ to separate the month and day from the year in a date

✔ to set off a word, phrase, or clause that interrupts the main thought of a sentence

✔ to separate a noun of direct address from the rest of the sentence

✔ to separate two or more adjectives which modify the same noun

✔ to enclose a title, name, or initials which follow a person's last name

✔ to separate an appositive or any other explanatory phrase from the rest of the sentence

✔ to separate two independent clauses in a compound sentence joined by such words as: but, or, for, so, yet

✔ to separate digits in a number greater than 999 except in street names and addresses.

✔ to make the meaning clear whenever necessary

## A hyphen is used . . .
✔ to divide a word at the end of a line (divide only between syllables)

✔ to join the words in compound numbers from twenty-one to ninety-nine and with fractions used as adjectives

✔ with the prefixes ex-, self-, all-, with the suffix -elect, and with all prefixes before a proper noun or proper adjective

✔ to prevent confusion or awkwardness

✔ to separate compound modifiers, two or more words expressing a single concept, when they precede a noun (for example, know-it-all attitude, or, full-time job)

## Dashes are used . . .
✔ to indicate an abrupt break in thought in the sentence

✔ to mean namely, in other words, that is, etc. before an explanation

✔ to use between numbers in a page reference

## A question mark is used . . .
✔ at the end of a direct question (an interrogative sentence)

✔ inside quotation marks when the quotation is a question

## An exclamation mark is used . . .
✔ after a word, phrase, or sentence that expresses strong feeling

✔ inside quotation marks when the quotation is an exclamation

## Quotation marks are used . . .
✔ to set off a direct quotation–a person's exact words (Single quotation marks are used for quotes within quotes)

✔ to enclose titles of chapters, articles, short stories, poems, songs and other parts of books and periodicals

✔ to set off slang and foreign words

## Underlining, or italics, is used . . .
✔ for titles of books, plays, magazines, newspapers, films, ships, radio and TV programs, music albums, works of art

✔ to emphasize words, letters, and figures referred to as such and for foreign words

# CAPITALIZATION & GRAMMAR GUIDE
### Use this quick reference chart to answer your grammatical questions

## Capitalize:

✔ the first word of every sentence

✔ all proper nouns and proper adjectives

✔ the first word in a direct quotation

✔ the first word in the greeting and the closing of a letter

✔ names of people and also the initials or abbreviations that stand for those names

✔ titles used with names of persons and abbreviations standing for those titles

✔ the first letter of all principal words in a title

✔ names of the days of the week, months of the year as well as special holidays

✔ names of languages, races, nationalities, religions, and proper adjectives formed from them

✔ all principal words in titles of books, periodicals, poems, stories, articles, movies, paintings and other works of art

✔ geographic names and sections of the country or world

✔ names of special events, historical events, government bodies, documents, and periods of time

✔ names of organizations, institutions, associations, teams, and their members

✔ names of businesses and brand names of their products

✔ abbreviations of titles and organizations

✔ words that refer to a specific deity and sacred books

✔ words denoting family relationships, as mother, father, brother, aunt, uncle, etc., only when these words stand for the name of the same individual

✔ use all caps for acronyms such as FBI, CIA, or NFL

## Punctuation Rules:

### A period is used . . .

✔ at the end of a declarative sentence as well as a mild imperative sentence

✔ after initials and abbreviations

✔ at the end of some rhetorical questions

✔ after numbers and letters in outlines

✔ inside quotation marks at the end of the sentence

✔ only once for sentences ending with an abbreviation

✔ as a decimal point and to separate dollars and cents

### A semicolon is used . . .

✔ to separate two independent clauses very close in meaning but not separated by and, but, or, nor, for, or yet

✔ to separate groups of words or phrases which already contain commas

✔ to connect two independent clauses when the second clause begins with a conjunctive adverb. (most of the time it is better to break the sentence into two separate parts)

### A colon is used . . .

✔ sometimes after the greeting of a formal letter

✔ before a list of items or details, especially after expressions like, "as follows" and "the following"

✔ before a long, formal statement or quotation

✔ between independent clauses when the second clause explains the first clause

✔ between the parts of a number which indicate time

### Parentheses are used . . .

✔ to enclose incidental explanatory matter which is added to a sentence but is not considered of major importance

✔ to enclose an author's insertion or comment

# Check Yourself

### Page 9, My New Companion
1. C, 2. D, 3. B, 4. A, 5. B

### Page 11, The Farm
1. A, 2. C, 3. A, 4. A, 5. B, 6. C, 7. False,
8. A, 9. C

### Page 13, Mountain Reminisce
1. B, 2. D, 3. C, 4. A, 5. B, 6. D, 7. C, 8. A

### Page 14, Thoraya
1. D, 2. B, 3. A

### Page 17, Christmas in a Grocery Store
1. The real meaning of Christmas is giving.
(answers may vary) 2. Sequence: 3, 2, 5, 1, 4, 6
3. Answers will vary. 4. a grocery store, 5. five
dollars, 6. pacifier and bib, 7. truck, 8. ham,
corn, yams, pack of rolls, 9. sharing or trading,
10. decline, 11. homonyms, 12. I, 13. out of the
store, into the parking lot, to an old brown
truck, 14. past, 15. direct object

### Page 19, Scarecrow
1. B, 2. acceptance, passage of time (answers
may vary), 3. A, 4. C, 5. D, 6. B, 7. A, 8. C, 9. D

### Page 21, Granddad
1. beaten down, worn out (answers will vary)
2. C, 3. eleven years old, 4. D, 5. Answers will
vary

### Page 22, An Ode to a Pond
1. B, 2. A, 3. C

### Page 24, Reflections on Pinewood Lake
1. C, 2. B, 3. A, 4. D, 5. C, 6. B, 7. A, 8. A, 9. D,
10. B

### Page 26, Lady of the Harbor
1. Statue of Liberty, 2. robe (answers may vary)
3. She welcomes people from other lands to
the U.S.A., land of the free. (answers may vary)
4. A, 5. Answers may vary.

### Page 28, The Scare in the Mountains
1. A, 2. B, 3. C, 4. D, 5. A, 6. D

### Page 29, A Dream
1. C, 2. B, 3. D, 4. A

### Page 31, The Calf
1. A, 2. C, 3. D, 4. B, 5. C, 6. B, 7. D, 8. A

### Page 33, Tiger Town
1. B, 2. C, 3. A, 4. D, 5. B, 6. C, 7. A, 8. A

### Page 35, Boom Boom's Turkey Farm
1. love and respect for ones grandparents
(answers may vary) 2. (answers may vary)
3. Sequence: 4, 2, 1, 6, 5, 3 4. C, 5. D,
6. 50 or 60, 7. delivers fish, 8. Billy Basham,
9. Belar Goodwin, 10. Grampa, 11. is

### Page 38, Mom at Bat
1. C, 2. D, 3. B, 4. B, 5. A, 6. B, 7. A, 8. D, 9. B

### Page 39, The Game
1. C, 2. B, 3. D

### Page 41, An Essay on the Grand Canyon
1. the Grand Canyon is a natural wonder of
the world (answers may vary) 2. you will
appreciate it more (answers may vary) ,
3. Sequence: 6, 3, 5, 1, 4, 2 4. C, 5. D, 6. 8,000 ft,
7. because the water comes from a large dam,
8. northern Arizona, 9. 1 day, 10. Answers may
vary

### Page 43, Help! I'm Lost
1. A, 2. C, 3. B, 4. B, 5. D, 6. B, 7. C.

### Page 46, The Race
1. A, 2. C, 3. A, 4. B, 5. D, 6. C, 7. B, 8. A, 9. D

### Page 48, What Really Happened to Jack?
1. a loud, sharp cry or sound, 2. to inflict pain
upon, 3. in a disorderly manner,
4. to bring or take, 5. to borrow eggs, 6. to run,
7. Jack Horner, 8. one week, 9. to resolve a misunderstanding Sequence: 4,1,3,5,6,2 10. went,
11. object of preposition, 12. we, 13. preposition, 14. pronoun

# CHECK YOURSELF, *continued*

**Page 50, The Canoe Trip**
1. B, 2. C, 3. B, 4. C, 5. A, 6. A, 7. B, 8. D.

**Page 51, The Turn of Her Life**
1. D, 2. A, 3. C, 4. B, 5. D, 6. A

**Page 53, Journal on Our Trip to N.Y.C.**
1. B, 2. D, 3. C, 4. A, 5. B, 6. D

**Page 55, The Pond**
1. to remember, 2. to think, 3. producing or having a melody, 4. to behave with courage and honor, 5. five years old, 6. within walking distance, 7. elm tree, 8. to relax and think, 9. yes, 10. his dad, 11. crickets and frogs, 12. Sequence: 2, 6, 4, 1, 5, 3 13. elm, 14. participial phrase, 15. are, 16. noun

**Page 57, New School**
1. D, 2. B, 3. C, 4. A, 5. C, 6. C, 7. B, 8. C, 9. D

**Page 58, All I Can See**
1. C, 2. B, 3. A, 4. D

**Page 60, The Canopy**
1. growing up, the power of imagination (answers may vary), 2. Answers may vary, 3. Sequence: 5, 3, 6, 4, 1, 2 4. floating down the Amazon, 5. 16, 6. Laura Ingalls, 7. 14, 8. Lilly, 9. adverb, 10. memories

**Page 61, My Favorite Spot**
1. C, 2. A, 3. A, 4. D, 5. C

**Page 63, My English Journal**
1. A, 2. B, 3. C, 4. D, 5. D, 6. B

**Page 65, A Visit**
1. there can be great satisfaction in helping others (answers may vary) 2. Sequence: 3, 5, 1, 4, 2 3. AIDS, 4. Belar's Landing, 5. to get his hair cut, 6. how great it was to be alive, 7. bearable, 8. visible, 9. pessimism, 10. torrential, 11. (answers may vary)

**Page 67, The Secret**
1. B, 2. A, 3. C, 4. D, 5. A, 6. B, 7. C, 8. D, 9. D, 10. A

**Page 69, Four-Wheeler Fishing Trip**
1. thinking and acting responsibly (answers may vary) 2. Sequence: 3, 4, 1, 5, 2 3. John, 4. Smith Lake, 5. it was left in neutral, 6. four-wheeler, 7. two groundhogs, 8. extremely annoying or irritating, 9. separated, 10. recognizing clearly, 11. Answers may vary

**Page 71, The Apple/Nightshade**
1. B, 2. A, 3. C, 4. D, 5. A, 6. B, 7. purple, orange and pink

**Page 74, Billy and the Butterfly**
1. B, 2. A, 3. C, 4. A, 5. A, 6. B, 7. C 8. D, 9. A, 10. C

**Page 76, The Sky**
1. B, 2. shimmer, 3. C, 4. wonder (answers may vary), 5. shimmering, 6. awesome (answers may vary), 7. see; to look at through ones eyes, to understand (answers may vary) 8. Answers may vary

**Page 78, An Exercise in Futility**
1. B, 2. B, 3. D, 4. C, 5. B, 6. D

**Page 80, Dozing**
1. B, 2. D, 3. all heads are dropped, 4. A, 5. C, 6. jab, 7. there's, 8. adverb

**Page 83, Friends**
1. friendship; learning to love oneself (answers may vary) 2. Sequence: 4, 5, 1, 3, 2 3. rescinded, 4. wanting something that is possessed by someone else (answers may vary), 5. reality, 6. the mall, 7. sentimental, 8. she stayed overnight at Angela's, 9. Manchester, 10. Insecure with one's own looks or self (answers may vary)

**Page 86, There's A Cannibal in My Backyard!**
1. because we have an imagination, we should never be bored (Answers may vary.) 2. Sequence: 5, 3, 2, 6, 1, 4, 7 3. mighty python, 4. Africa, 5. lioness, 6. exploration and adventure, 7. cannibals, 8. A, 9. B, 10. C, 11. D

**Page 88, Fate Over Chocolate Pie**
Essay content may vary

# CHECK YOURSELF, *continued*